THE LITTLE GIRL WHO LIVES DOWN THE LANE

THE LITTLE GIRL WHO LIVES DOWN THE LANE

Laird Koenig

Coward, McCann & Geoghegan

New York

For permission to quote from copyrighted material the author wishes to thank the following:

Warner Bros. Music, Inc., for portions of "Tea For Two" by Vincent Youmans and Irving Caesar. Copyright © 1924 by HARMS, Inc. Copyright renewed. All rights reserved. Used by permission of Warner Bros. Music, Inc.

Harvard University Press and the Trustees of Amherst College for portions of "There's a Certain Slant of Light" and "An Awful Tempest Mashed the Air" by Emily Dickinson, reprinted by permission of the publishers and the Trustees of Amherst College from Thomas H. Johnson, Editor, *The Poems of Emily Dickinson*, Cambridge, Massachusetts: The Belknap Press of Harvard University Press. Copyright © 1951, 1955 by the President and Fellows of Harvard College.

Little, Brown and Company, Inc. for an excerpt from "That Love Is All There Is" by Emily Dickinson, from Thomas H. Johnson, Editor, *The Complete Poems of Emily Dickinson*, Copyright © 1914, 1942 by Martha Dickinson Bianchi.

For Mary and Richard Kebbon

1

It was the kind of evening the little girl liked best.

She stood at the window on this last night of October and looked out on the world shivering on the edge of winter. Cold wind rattled the dead flower stalks in the garden and scraped the maples' naked branches, sending the last of their dry leaves flying like torn black paper into the dark. Suddenly the girl pulled the window curtains and closed out the night.

She ran on bare feet to a stone fireplace and with an iron poker prodded the logs till the red coals crackled into a blaze. She held out her hands to the fire's glow and felt it reaching out into the sitting room and kitchen of what had been, until a hundred years ago, a farmhouse. The owner of the house had put a new gas heater against the wall, but the girl loved the warmth of a fire and the sharp smoke-smell of burning maple logs.

A few more steps took her around a coffee table and a rocking chair to the gleaming metal dials of a stereo. She raised the volume and sound flooded down from speakers hanging above in the shadows of the rafters. Liszt's Piano Concerto Number One and one of the world's great symphony orchestras swelled and throbbed into every corner till it seemed the tiny house itself was the orchestra. The glorious sound wrapped around her till her heart and the music beat as one. She raised the volume and the music soared even higher.

No neighbor would telephone or pound on the door to complain of the noise. The nearest neighbor lived a quarter of a mile down the lane filled with dead leaves.

The girl stood motionless in the middle of the room. She waited in the near dark as dim red light flickering from the fire wavered the shadows back into the corners.

She waited. Soon the moment for which she had waited so many days would come.

From early morning, except for her walk in the autumn rain into the village, she had cleaned the house. Down on her hands and knees she had waxed the oak floor. She had dusted and polished the unpainted wood surface of the simple furniture which twice during September had brought an antique dealer, a man in skin-fitting black leather who smelled of cloves, to the house with increasing offers to buy everything in sight. When her father explained that most of these pieces were not his to sell, the dealer had shaken his head sadly. They were, he said—his eyes making love to the table and chairs, the candlesticks, the couch, the braided rug—some of the best examples of Early American he had ever seen. The floor and the furniture, already polished by the years, now shone in the firelight. Even the braided rug under the gateleg table, said to be a hundred and fifty years old, was almost restored to its colors since the girl had taken it outside and beaten it free of dust. In the kitchen, separated by a wooden counter, the metal of a modern range and refrigerator glinted in the fire's glow.

At the kitchen counter the girl opened a paper cake box

and with both hands carefully lifted a small cake thick with pale yellow frosting onto a plate. Although snowy sugar daubed her hands, she did not lick her fingers. She rubbed off the frosting with a paper towel.

Into the cake's gleaming, rippled-satin surface she slowly pushed thirteen tiny yellow candles, standing them upright in a ring. The other candles she returned to a drawer. She struck a wooden match, the first of three it would take, moving the flame as quickly as she was able, to bring all thirteen candles alive and dancing with fire. When she shook the match to kill the flame, her hand silhouetted by the blaze of candlelight, glowed red. She studied it for a long moment just as she had looked at everything more closely on this special day. Slowly she turned her hand. Her fingers, blood red at the edges, were almost transparent except for the line of small, perfectly trimmed fingernails.

She carried the dazzling cake, but instead of taking it directly into the parlor, she crossed to the dark corner by the front door where, under a coatrack, a long mirror glinted. Even before she reached the mirror the candle glow blazed the shadowy corner into light.

She stood very still before the doubled spangle of flames. In the wavering candlelight her hands and face seemed pale, white as wax. Her long hair, which was usually the color of fallen oak leaves, was now touched with copper. She stared. She decided it was true, her face *was*, as her father had written in one of his poems, heart shaped. Certainly the brow was wide, the chin pointed. White and heart shaped and dotted with freckles that seemed darker in the firelight, dots from a crayon on white paper. Her eyes sparkled, full of wild light. Small eyes, she thought. Green but small. Once she had complained to her father that other girls her age had enormous eyes. Her father, translating a Russian poem at the time, had put down his work and insisted that her eyes weren't small at all. He explained at what was, now that she thought about it, too great length, that she had fine bones and a face which had already grown to its full size. Her eyes were now *exactly* right for the size of her face.

At the time she had known this was her father's love for her talking. She had not been convinced. Even then. Her eyes were small. Instead of small green eyes, even wildly flashing and full of light as they were now, she wished she had great, big, enormous eyes.

"Happy Birthday," she said to the girl in the mirror. She was careful not to smile, for a smile would show her chipped front tooth and she could not bear that. "Happy Birthday to me," she said and any worries about her eyes— and they *were* green and she loved that—paled in comparison to the agony she felt over the chipped tooth. Abruptly she told herself, very sternly, not to think about the tooth, not to let it spoil this special day. Slowly as one in a cere- mony, she carried the blaze of candlelight away from the mirror. Music throbbed around her, and the night wind tearing at the house soon filled her with a joy so great she closed her eyes trying to hold in her happiness, to keep this moment from passing.

At the coffee table where she knelt to place the cake be- fore the fire, she could almost see herself performing some ritual act, something out of a play or one of those old Biblical movies she had seen on the BBC. She could see—almost as if she were outside herself—a slender little girl in a long, white-linen caftan her father had bought for her in Morocco. This, the finest thing she owned, had blue embroidery at the collar and sleeves, a color which would keep her safe, the shopkeeper had assured both father and daughter, from the evil eye. Her feet were bare on the smooth oak floor. Yes, she was quite satisfied. She looked very much like one of those solemn virgins in mythology, a priestess placing an offering on an altar.

She tucked her bare feet under her legs and stared into the candle flames. She reached behind her, and with her hand, set the chair rocking. Again she shut her eyes, feeling herself part of the fire's warmth, the candle flames, the music, the night wind.

Suddenly at a sound she held her breath. She sprang to her feet and lowered the music's volume.

Thuds pounded on the door.

She ran and parted the front window curtains and peered out. In the windy night a tall man in a raincoat stood at the door. Lit by a strange orange light, he seemed to glow and waver like the candles on her cake.

She knew more knocks were coming, thuds she dreaded, and suddenly she wanted nothing more than to reach the front door in time to stop them. Before she had reached the hall they came, three bangs, even louder than she expected.

"Yes?" she asked at the door.

"Mr. Jacobs?" The voice on the other side, out in the night, was unknown to the girl.

"Who is it?" Her accent was English.

"Frank Hallet."

"Hallet." The name meant nothing to her. Hallet? Then she remembered the real-estate woman who had leased the house to her father. Hallet. He must be her son. What could he possibly want? The girl stood motionless. She knew the man would not go away till she had opened the door.

"Just a minute," she called.

She raced back to the coffee table and opened a cigarette box. From a package of Gauloise, she drew out a cigarette and holding back her long hair, leaned into the flames of the birthday cake. The tip of the cigarette glowed, as she drew on the cigarette. Rising, she turned and blew the smoke behind her. Repeating her smoking, she sent smoke into the four corners of the room, before hurling the cigarette into the fireplace and running back to the hall.

She turned the lock and opened the door on the night and the wind that sent leaves scratching across the oak floor.

The man glowed in the dark because he held one of those pumpkins she had seen lying gold and orange in the fields and for sale in stacks at the crossroads. This great orange globe had been scooped hollow and a burning candle within shone out through two eyes, a nose, and an enormous grinning gash of a mouth cut through the thick pumpkin flesh.

"Trick or treat." The man's voice boomed, almost a shout so he could be heard above the wind.

"What?" the girl asked. But it was not because she could not hear. She stared at the man. Cold air swept into the house.

What did he want?

"Trick or treat." The man thrust the grinning pumpkin face at her as if his demand could be explained by the blazing eyes, the fiery smile.

"I'm sorry," the girl said. She groped unsuccessfully for some way to show him she did not understand why he was here or what he wanted. She made no effort to conceal her shivering. The precious moment she had worked toward all day, like the warmth in the house, was draining away into the cold. More than anything else at this moment she wished, longed, ached for some way to make this man leave her door.

"Halloween," the man shouted the way he might try to communicate with a foreigner who did not speak his language.

"Yes?" the girl said, wondering if she dared put her hand on the door frame, a move that would block the one step which would bring him from the porch through the door.

The man moved before she did. Only one step, but already he was leaning into the hall, peering into the sitting room.

"Somebody's birthday?" he was staring at the candles glowing on the cake.

Inside the long sleeves of her caftan, the little girl's hands tightened into fists.

"*Your* birthday?" the man asked.

The girl nodded slowly. Under her sleeves she opened her fists only to rub her arms against the cold.

"Happy Birthday."

"Thank you," she said flatly, striving to bleed the two syllables of any feeling, for now she felt her only weapon against this man was to give him absolutely no encouragement beyond the barest civility. She thought of older women in London in stores like Harrods and tea shops like Richoux who could freeze clerks and waitresses with their marvelous studied iciness. If she could succeed in creating that kind of chill, the man would be forced to go away.

"May I tell my father what you want?"

"Besides your birthday, tonight's also Halloween," he almost shouted.

Did he not think she could hear him? Again the little girl thought of London and a friend of her father's, an old poet with filthy hair, who in spite of living in one tiny room— hardly big enough to hold his clutter of old cups of half-drunk tea in which cigarette butts floated, much less the yellowing books and torn manuscripts and the smell of cats —forever roared in a voice that was as loud and flat as this man's. After their first visit her father had explained that his elderly friend was deaf.

"Halloween. Trick or treat." The man repeated the words carefully in case the wind carried them away.

Though the girl showed him a face as expressionless and unencouraging as her voice, he seemed to feel a need to explain.

"My name's Hallet. Frank Hallet. Your father knows me."

The man twisted around to peer into the dark where the wind scattered the leaves.

"My two kids will be by any minute. Trick or treating. Right now they're up the lane at your neighbor's waiting for the candied apples to harden. What I'm doing is I'm sort of acting as an advance scout. To make sure any houses they try to trick or treat don't have any *real* goblins." The man giggled.

The girl was certain she had never heard such a silly sound come from a grown man. His face, reflecting the orange candle glow, searched hers. That was a joke. It could be taken two ways. Did she understand his real meaning?

"Like dirty old men who try to give candy to pretty little girls, right?"

He giggled again.

The girl was beginning to think her expressionless mask was a mistake. The man seemed compelled to make himself understood.

"You'd be surprised," he said. "Some pretty creepy people. Even right here in the village."

The wind lifted long strands of his brown hair revealing a bald head that gleamed like her polished furniture. Undaunted by the little girl's impassiveness, Hallet began to explain the significance of this particular cold and windy evening.

"At Halloween we trick or treat. You still don't understand? You're English, right?"

"Yes."

"You don't have Halloween in England?"

"No."

"Hey," he said, "we're letting all the heat out." The man thrust himself inside the door, a second step that forced the little girl back into the hall.

"Tell your father you've got company."

"TELL YOUR FATHER," the man had said as he pushed himself and his glowing pumpkin into her home. "Tell your father," he had said as if he need not ask her permission to enter, as if this was not the girl's home, but only her father's.

She stood motionless at the front door and with a great deal more hatred than most men and women remember that children can feel, clamped her teeth and held her silence as the man's wet shoes splotched footprints across the shining oak planks of her polished floor. At the window he shoved back the curtain and shaded his eyes to look out through the glass.

"Your neighbors are too far for the kids to hear me call," he said, his breath misting the window she had washed that afternoon. "But from here I can watch for them. One's dressed up like Frankenstein's monster. The other one's a green skeleton." Pretending to shiver with fright, he giggled.

The girl hated his giggle, and she hated the smell of cologne, sweet and heavy, that he left behind him. Choking with rage, all she could think to do was slam the door.

She remained in the hall, staring at him.

He was taller than her father. His puffy red face glowed from the cold wind. That bitter wind might account for blue eyes being so watery, but those eyes had a look she had seen in the eyes of a friend of her father's, another poet her father said drank too much. Finding the girl staring at him, the man put the pumpkin down on the gateleg table and with his left hand, on which an unusually large gold wedding band glinted, smoothed his hair while with the other he drew a chapstick from his raincoat pocket and ran glistening balm over his large, red lips. Like the trail of slime left by a snail, thought the girl.

He slipped the ointment back into his raincoat pocket, the edges of which were filthy with grease. The same black bordered the sleeves and the bottom of the coat. His gray flannel trousers below, hung unpressed over the wet brown-suede shoes that had tracked the floor. The pink hand continued to smooth strings of brown hair across his scalp that shone under the hair's inadequate cover. Everything about the man seemed soiled, shiny or red.

"If you're going to live in the States," he said in a voice that was still far too loud, "you have to know about Halloween. That's because tonight's the night all the kids get dressed up, come by your door with masks and pumpkins."

The girl, who had yet to move from the hall, clawed her hand on the door knob.

"When they come to your door," the man said, "they holler 'trick or treat' and you're supposed to act scared. If you don't give them a treat they pull some terrible trick on you." He waggled a red finger at her and giggled. "Something dire."

The man pressed his pink face back to the window to peer out into the night. His breath made another dim little patch of fog on the black glass.

"As for being so terrible and dire," he said, "I wouldn't

worry too much about that. With my two kids it's only as dire as four- and six-year-olds can get."

The girl could not imagine this tall pink man with the heavy wedding ring as the father of two children. Compared to her own father he seemed more like a child himself than a parent. A child who smelled of cologne.

"Now you understand? About trick or treat?"

"What's considered a treat?"

"Popcorn. Candy. Anything."

"Would they like a piece of cake?"

Both the man and the girl looked at the cake glowing with candles in front of the fire. A few of the tiny candles had already burned down and their flames had died. Others flickered.

"But that's birthday cake," the man said.

The girl left the front door to go into the kitchen area. A drawer opened, a cupboard door slammed. With a knife and a box of waxed paper, she knelt before the cake.

"You shouldn't," Hallet said.

"Shouldn't what?" asked the girl who had already drawn a careful line with the tip of the blade across the satiny frosting.

"Cut it. Just for them I mean."

"They won't like it?"

"Sure, but . . ." In front of his raincoat a red hand rose in half protest, but it fell.

"Pretty cake."

The girl drew the knife through the snowfield of pale yellow.

He turned to glance through the window. Then suddenly he spoke, "Where's your mother?"

The girl frowned, concentrating on cutting the cake. The man waited. Was she not going to answer his question? She was lifting out the first wedge of cake when she spoke.

"My mother's dead."

"But your father's here though." The man sniffed the air exaggerating his reaction to what he sensed. "He smokes French cigarettes, right?"

The girl ripped a long piece of waxed paper from the box, spread it flat and carefully wrapped the first piece of cake.

"Am I right? About the French cigarettes?"

"Yes."

The finger of his red hand waggled. "And he's a *very* wicked man."

The girl, cutting the second wedge, did not look up.

"French cigarettes. Ho, ho." The man's wicked chuckle included the girl into his mythology, the folklore that anything, even cigarettes, if French, was sinful. He giggled again. "French cigarettes. Out here on the Island? *Off* season? *Very* wicked." His innuendo seemed incomplete without another conspiratorial chuckle.

The girl wrapped the second piece of cake. With the knife she scraped the snowy frosting from her fingers, but she did not eat it.

"My father's not at all wicked. He's a poet."

She was looking into the circle of flames on the candles which yet burned.

"Upstairs?" asked the man.

She gazed across the flames at the man at the window.

"Who?"

"Your father."

"No," she said. "In his study. Working."

"A poet."

"Yes."

"My mother says he's a poet, too, and when my mother says anything—well, automatically it has to be true. It wouldn't dare not be. My mother's the real-estate lady who leased your father this house."

The girl rose from the oak floor and carried the two pieces of wrapped cake to the man at the window.

At his strong scent she felt a wave of nausea rise.

"The kids are going to love that," he said reaching for the offering. His red hands touched the girl's slender white fingers. Almost dropping the cake, she pulled her hands away.

For too long a moment the man found the girl staring at his hands. Hands. According to her father, hands told more about a person than a face, and these hands were small and soft as a woman's and even though they were pink and red with cold, the backs were dotted with large pores like a pigskin wallet her father had once been given as a gift, but had thrown away because the leather had never lost its unpleasant smell. The little girl was certain that if this man's touched her again her flesh would jump on her bones.

"Clearing up," the man said. "No more rain tonight. Just mud puddles for the kids to splash through."

The girl returned to the coffee table, picked up the knife and waxed paper, and carried them into the kitchen.

"So quiet," he said, and for the first time his voice was hushed. "Listen. Sometimes from this house you can hear the ocean. Tonight all you can hear is the wind."

From the kitchen the girl watched the man across the room at the window.

"Most people think it gets lonely out here in the winter," he said, wiping the patch of mist with his raincoat sleeve. "Actually you and your father are lucky to be here this time of year. As soon as fall comes all the summer people pack up, put up the shutters and dash back to New York and turn on the steam heat. Winter comes and all the Jews finally give the place back to the natives. Back to us Wasps. *And* the Wops."

The man was now looking at the birthday cake candles burning down, one by one winking out. "You're thirteen?"

"No."

"Then why thirteen candles?"

"All I had."

"You're fourteen?"

"My father published his first poem when he was only eleven."

"In England, right?"

"Yes."

"It's easier to be a poet in England." A red hand slid across his hair, rearranging it over the shining bald patch on his skull. "Here in America when you're eleven it's Little League."

Could he not tell she did not want to talk?

"I wrote poetry," he said. "In prep school. For the school paper. You write poetry?"

"Yes."

"What about?"

She shrugged. It was the least possible answer she could give to his question. Why did he go on talking? Nothing seemed to deter him.

"Published?" he did not seem at all discouraged by her silence. "Your poetry?"

She nodded.

"School paper?"

In the kitchen the girl shut a drawer but did not answer.

"Newspapers? Magazines?"

In the fireplace a log burned through and fell, rolling burning coals onto the hearth. The girl ran from the kitchen to pick up the iron poker.

"I'd like to read your poems some time."

The girl poked the embers back into the fireplace.

"Your father's name is Leslie Jacobs, right?"

"Yes."

"Yours?"

"Rynn."

"R-Y-N-N? That's very unusual."

The girl pushed a glowing coal under the grate.

"You must be very bright." He looked around the room. "Just you and your father live here?"

She did not reply but lifted the lid of the woodbox and dropped the poker back inside it.

"Just you two?" The man asked again.

"Yes."

Hallet moved to the rocker and with a red hand set it rocking.

"His chair?"

"Yes."

"And you don't like for anyone else to sit in it, right?"

The girl shrugged in the direction of the man who pressed strands of brown hair against his skull.

"Vibes," he said. "*Vibrations*, I get about things. Am I right?" With the back of his pigskin hand he stopped the chair's rocking. "Some people have a superstition about rocking a chair when no one's in it."

The girl did not turn from the fire.

"They have that one in England? Now don't try to tell me you're not superstitious."

Silence.

"You *should* be superstitious," he said. "After all, it *is* Halloween. You should also have a black cat. Black cat's practically obligatory for tonight." He glanced around as if to show the girl he expected to find a cat here in spite of her denial. "No cat at all?"

"No cat."

"All little girls love cats."

The girl crossed to a corner by the woodbox and knelt down to open a tiny wire-mesh cage.

"What have you got there?" The creature the girl held in her hands was the man's excuse to edge nearer.

"White rat?"

As Hallet maneuvered for a closer look at the rat, she turned her face from his scent.

"What's your name?" he asked of the rat.

The little girl kissed the rat's pink nose.

"*Got* to have a name. Come on, Rynn. Tell me what it is."

"Gordon," but the girl was talking to the tiny creature whose whiskers twitched, not to the man.

"English?"

Rynn nodded. She had not even told her father when she smuggled Gordon into the States in her Marks and Spencer duffle coat. After another kiss for Gordon, she carried the rat to the table and set him down before the cake. The rat raised his head and his pink eyes surveyed the mountain of pale yellow frosting, the candles wavering with flames. Rynn picked up a crumb and held it to the rat to nibble. Her eyes sparkled with candlelight. Gordon stood up, his front claws sinking into the frosting.

"Before the candles all go out, shouldn't you call your father?"

"Not when he's working."

The man watched the girl and Gordon for a long, silent moment. "Anybody ever tell you you're a very pretty girl? Pretty hair. Especially in the candlelight." His hand reached out but stopped short of touching Rynn's hair.

"Pretty girl like you—on your birthday and all—no boyfriends?"

The girl and her pet, in a world together, closed out the man. She leaned over the table to put her face close to Gordon.

Hallet studied her shining hair, the caftan that stretched tight across her back and over her hips.

"Come on. I'll bet you've got a boyfriend. Lots of boyfriends. Pretty girl like you."

Suddenly the man reached down and slapped the girl on the curve of her buttocks. Rynn wheeled around to face him, her eyes glaring hate.

Hallet giggled nervously. "It's okay. I get to spank you. On your birthday you *have* to get spanked. Once for each year. And then one to grow on."

Rynn's green eyes held the man's until he slid his glance away.

"It's a game," he protested. "A birthday game!" His voice was loud and shrill. Backing up toward the gateleg table, he almost stumbled.

"You think. . . . Wow. Look, I've got two kids of my own. Out there." He retreated to the window and peered out.

"Hey, here comes the green skeleton now! *And* Frankenstein's monster!" His cry was almost jubilant as he moved past the table and scooped up the glowing pumpkin. He shoved the wrapped cake into his raincoat pocket mashing the two slices. "Thanks for the treat. I guarantee my monsters' best behavior. No tricks."

With long steps, Hallet backed toward the door.

"Tell your father I'm sorry I missed him."

He flung open the door. Outside two costumed children waited in the blowing leaves.

"I almost forgot. Happy Birthday!"

But Rynn did not thank the man. With another glare surprisingly full of hate, she faced him.

Hallet giggled and hurried out the door.

"Happy Birthday!" he boomed, but the wind hurled his voice into the night.

The girl shut the door and turned the lock.

FRIDAY MIGHT have been a day in spring; the air
was that soft under a cloudless blue sky. By afternoon, however, it felt more like fall. The air was sharp with wood
smoke; the clapboard farmhouse behind its screen of tree
branches was bathed in a light more amber than golden,
and shadows that grow as long only when the year is dying
stretched across the dead leaves.

A 1966 drophead Bentley, huge and shining and of such
a rich dark red the villagers called it "liver-colored," moved
down the lane through the drifting smoke and slowed to a
stop in front of the house.

In a silence broken only by crows cawing, a car door
opened, and a woman who was older than she looked from
a distance left the car with a basket. Her hair, touched by
the sunlight, shone gold, but a gold with a hard, unnatural
glint. She slammed the heavy door, locked it, and pulled
a brown tweed coat around her. Her hands, even in the full
light, were as unlined and pink as those of the man who had
come to the house on Halloween. This rosy plumpness, the
same as Frank Hallet's, kept her face smooth except for two

deep frown lines converging at the bridge of her nose like painted Hindu markings. Hard blue eyes glittered, polished stones peering from the pink, smooth face.

Fitting the wicker basket over her arm, the woman strode toward the house, brown suede shoes crunching acorns and scattering dry leaves.

Overhead, in the branches of a leafless tree, a blue jay flashed. In a far-off field crows cawed. Even further away, ocean waves churned on the shore.

Halfway up the walk the woman slowed to listen, for the windows and doors of the house ahead stood open as if breathing in the autumn air. Strange sounds brought her to a complete stop.

She could hear voices intoning words and phrases, but even straining to listen she could make no sense of them nor guess what language they might be.

Instead of going to the front door, the woman made her way through the leaves to the back of the house and a small untended garden. Here the grass was high. Chrysanthemums, yellow and orange, survived, but zinnias and dahlias, black and rotting, drooped on brittle stalks.

In a grape arbor the woman found shriveled clusters of raisins furred with mold. An espaliered apple tree, crucified against the wall of the house, bore a few yellow apples, but these were either pockmarked with wormholes or brown with rot.

"They really might have sprayed," she said to herself.

Only the quinces in the sprawl of a fallen bush were plump, green and gold. Reaching out, she snapped off the choicest of the fruit. In no time she filled her basket.

She stepped through the dry grass to the house to examine the clapboard siding. Some of the wood, silver-gray with the years, was split and crumbling. At a window a shutter hung unevenly on a rusted hinge. The woman made a mental note to call the handyman in the village, but in the next instant the landlady in her nature decided the little house could wait till spring.

At the open window the voices were louder, more distinct and even more unfathomable.

"Ha-oo-KHAL luh-tal-PAYN mee POH?"

Another voice, much quieter, repeated:

"Ha-oo-KHAL luh-tal-PAYN mee POH."

The woman peered in the window. To her surprise she had never seen the little parlor and kitchen so clean. The polished furniture and the oak floor shone; the pewter candlesticks on the gateleg table gleamed in the sunlight.

"Ha-too-KHAL luh tal-PAYN a-voo-REE?"

The woman realized one of the voices was too loud to be anything but an amplified voice from a phonograph record. But the other?

"Ha-too-KHAL luh tal-PAYN a-voo-REE?"

The response was coming from the dark corner by the fireplace. Because she could not see into the corner, the woman returned to the front of the house and the windows, and from here saw the little girl, who had been sitting stroking a white rat as she intoned the words, rise quickly, slip the animal back into his mesh cage, and run to the phonograph.

"A-va-KAYSH see KHAH muh-ko-MEET, mees-PAHR—"

With the sound off, it was quiet enough that she heard crows in the autumn sunlight.

Rynn ran barefoot to the front door, but the woman with the basket pushed past her, her rough tweed coat brushing the girl as she entered the house. She held up the basket.

"Quinces. I've always thought they looked like lumpy apples."

Glancing around for some place to put them, she chose to set the quinces on the gateleg table in the sitting room.

"How are you two getting along out here?" she asked, smoothing gold hair that did not need smoothing, hair that crackled with hair spray. "Everything all right?"

"Fine," Rynn said, wondering where she had seen hair of this same unnatural sheen.

"The new gas heater keeping you two cosy enough?"

"Lovely."

"Good." The woman's sharp eyes darting around the parlor snapped to Rynn, who found them a colder blue than Frank Hallet's. They appraised the girl from head to foot. If the woman disapproved of the youngster's black turtleneck sweater, Levis, or bare feet, she said nothing. Apparently she felt the need to introduce herself.

"I'm Cora Hallet. Your father leased this house from me."

"We met in your office."

"That's right," the woman said, her eyes flickering back to the room, the landlady inspecting her domain. At the rocking chair she paused to run a questioning hand over the back.

"Where did this come from?"

"It's my father's."

Mrs. Hallet glanced at the chair, then at the coffee table.

"Don't mind me," she said dragging the chair back into a corner and filling its place with the table from the fireplace. "But the table belongs here."

The woman glanced around again as if certain she would find more changes she would have to put right.

"Can't *stand* things out of place." As she spoke she smiled in an effort to soften the authority with which she made her moves. But she was already at the couch plumping and bringing the bunched cushions into a precise row.

She frowned. A pewter tankard on the fireplace mantel

seemed to demand examination. She took it down, turned it over to study the touchmark. From her tweed coat she drew eyeglasses that dangled on a gold chain and fitting them, sparkling in the light, over her face, said: "English?"

"Yes."

"His?"

"My father's."

"Not a bad piece, but wrong for this room."

The girl wondered if the woman could see the rage that was beginning to seethe within her. She felt her face must be scarlet.

"That table and the braided rug, they belong against the wall."

The woman turned and smiled again.

"I know," she said holding the smile, "you're going to tell me that poets aren't supposed to live like other people. That it?"

Rynn's green eyes never left the woman who, instead of waiting for an answer, picked up a book from the mantel, a thin volume bound in gray.

"One of his?"

"Yes," said the girl.

She examined the binding, apparently unimpressed.

"I keep forgetting to have him autograph it for me."

The woman fanned the book's leaves. She stopped.

"This one already is." She adjusted her glasses. " 'I love you,' Signed 'Father.' How very nice."

Mrs. Hallet closed the book with a snap and slid the volume back onto the mantelpiece. "And it's nice to have a famous poet in the village, except none of us ever sees so much as a glimpse of him."

She picked up a tiny bouquet of straw flowers.

"English?"

The girl nodded. In her anger, she did not know if she could control herself to speak.

At the woman's touch, dry petals sifted to the mantelpiece. "We don't even see you two at the market." Her eyebrows raised, her silent comment, her judgment on the English father and daughter's behavior.

"The market delivers," Rynn said as calmly as she was able.

Mrs. Hallet's eyebrows held their arch. She spoke slowly, like a teacher presenting a fact she had decided was new for the child, new and difficult to grasp. "If one can afford it." She drew a box of cigarettes from her pocket, lit one, and turned to the open window and frowned at the grape arbor.

Rynn had decided what the color of the woman's hair made her think of. Since it was so obviously dyed, the girl wondered why the woman chose a color which did not exist in nature but only in the spun gold of those wretched little creatures in toy shops called Barbie Dolls.

"That is *exactly* the color," she said to herself. "Barbie-Doll hair on an old woman."

"Did you want me to give my father a message?"

The woman still gazed out the window.

"It's such a shame there are so few grapes this year. Only takes a bit of spraying. . . ." She unbuttoned her brown tweed coat, making herself comfortable, expecting to stay. Rynn, who was not going to ask her if she wished a cup of tea, would not have been surprised had the woman asked for one.

Barbie-Doll hair. Lipstick that was too red, a blood-red slash, pulled smoke from her cigarette.

"It's not that I'm so absolutely wild about quince jam, but I simply can't bear to see anything go to waste. That is undoubtedly the Puritan in me."

Rynn waited for the woman to exhale, but the smoke seemed to stay inside the pink face.

"So very fashionable these days to *talk* about waste. Ecology and pollution are all the thing. You'll notice, however, no one *does* one single thing about it."

Ash had grown long on the cigarette and Rynn brought an ashtray in which Mrs. Hallet ground out her cigarette.

"I can give my father any message."

"I came," Mrs. Hallet said, "to get the jelly glasses. For as long as I can remember Edith Wilson and I have been making jelly from those grapes. We stored last year's glasses in the cellar."

She turned from the window to find the girl staring at her.

"Your father's not home?"

"No."

"Don't tell me he's actually making an appearance in the village."

"New York."

"When I was outside I could have sworn I heard voices."

At the phonograph, Mrs. Hallet lifted the plastic cover from the turntable. Her plump fingers picked up the disc.

Rynn shut her eyes against her rage. She fought an all but overwhelming impulse to tell the woman to keep her fat, greasy fingers off the record.

Rattling her glasses on their gold chain to balance them across the crease in her brow, Mrs. Hallet leaned close to the record to read.

"Hebrew?"

Incapable of speech the girl nodded.

Mrs. Hallet clattered the record back onto the turntable. "I should think French would be more help. *Or* Italian. Lord knows there are enough of *them* around here these days to speak it with."

The girl surprised herself by saying, "Would you like to write out a message for my father?"

Pink fingers riffled through a stack of record albums that leaned against the wall.

"So many outsiders in the village these days," the woman sighed deeply, then flicked on her smile. "You'll have to forgive me, but you see there've been Hallets out here on the Island for more than three hundred years." The woman left the stereo unit to run her hand over the couch's glazed chintz.

"This couch belongs over there." A stubby finger pointed at the window.

At the gateleg table Mrs. Hallet picked up a newspaper. "English?"

"Yes."

The glasses went back to the crease in her brow as she studied the folded paper. "I adore crosswords."

"Take it with you if you like."

Pulling off her glasses, she turned to the girl.

"But your father is doing it."

"I'm doing it."

She arched an eyebrow in mock astonishment. "*And* Hebrew. You are brilliant." She turned a few pages in the paper and tossed it onto the table.

The little girl refolded the paper, the puzzle on top.

"My son's children told me that on Halloween you gave them birthday cake."

"Yes."

"That was very generous of you."

"Your son said it was called 'trick or treat.'"

The woman moved one of the pewter candlesticks on the table a few inches to stand in a precise line with its mate.

"He came inside the house?"

"Who?" asked Rynn, although she knew who the woman was talking about.

Mrs. Hallet readjusted her glasses for a close examination of the pewter, as if she expected to find scratches.

"My son," she said.

"Yes," said the girl. "He came in."

"Your father," the woman was making an effort to seem to care more about the pewter than whatever the girl might answer. "Your father *was* here that evening?"

"My father was in his study."

"Working?"

"Translating. When he's translating he can't be disturbed."

"Of course." Mrs. Hallet turned from the table, her hand touching the rocking chair, bringing it to life.

"Since that evening, has my son come back?" She maintained the pretense that her interest was not in the answer; she was merely making the small talk of one neighbor calling on another.

"No," said the girl, her eyes still on the woman.

"Hasn't been back at all?"

"No."

Mrs. Hallet caressed the rocker's polished wood.

"If my son *should* come back and your father isn't here . . ." She examined the wood's smooth grain trying to make what she said continue to sound casual. "If he *should* come back, perhaps, in that case, it might be better if you didn't let him in."

"He didn't ask my permission that time."

"I hope," said Mrs. Hallet with considerable iciness, "you didn't intend that to sound quite so rude."

Rynn knew the woman expected a denial of any intention of rudeness. Like the cup of tea, she was not going to get it.

"I'll tell my father you said not to let your son in the door."

"That won't be necessary." The woman's eyes flashed with anger.

"Perhaps I don't understand what it is you want."

"One thing I certainly do *not* want is to go on and on about something that doesn't matter in the slightest. I came for the jelly glasses."

The girl's silence seemed an accusation.

"We'll get them now," the woman said.

"You don't want me to tell my father about your son?"

"I said that would be enough. This is something I don't expect you to understand."

"He thinks I have pretty hair. He tell you that?"

The woman's pink knuckles went white as she gripped the back of the rocker.

In this instant Rynn dared to raise her eyes and look straight into the woman's. Rynn knew the woman was wondering exactly how wise she might be.

Mrs. Hallet cleared her throat and squared her shoulders.

"I'd like the jelly glasses now."

"I haven't seen them."

"I told you, they're down in the cellar."

Rynn's eyes faltered.

"We move the table so I can take up the rug and raise the trapdoor. You *do* understand *that*, don't you?" The voice was becoming harsher. *"The glasses are down in the cellar!"*

Rynn buried her fists under the waist of her black sweater.

"Take your side of the table."

"My father and I like the table where it is!"

"This table *belongs* against the wall!"

A silence that lasted a full ten seconds separated them.

"You will forgive me," Mrs. Hallet said, etching each word with acid, "but when I was your age I was taught to do as a grown person said!"

Rynn shut her eyes on the red rage she must not allow to explode.

"I'm sorry, Mrs. Hallet—"

"I came to get those glasses."

"I'll get them for you later."

But the woman refused to hear anything more.

"*Move this table!*"

"This is *my* house!"

"You are an extraordinarily rude little girl who is going to do precisely as I say!"

Rynn waited. Would the woman grab her shoulders and thrust her to the table? The pink face flushed magenta with fury. Angry veins stood out on her neck like purple cords. In this moment Rynn realized Mrs. Hallet was incapable of speech. To her great surprise she found herself shouting at her.

"Last week you took the only good grapes we had! I saw you! And now the quinces! You never asked if you might. Not about those either!"

Mrs. Hallet's red mouth fell open only to shut with a snap. Then she lashed back.

"The Wilsons' grapes! The Wilsons' quinces!"

"Today, you didn't ask if you might—you walked bang into my house!"

"The *Wilsons'* house!"

"*My* house!"

"*Leased!*" The woman with the gold hair spat out the word. She took the moment this gave her to gasp a few deep breaths, and still shaking with rage, she managed to speak without the rawness of hysteria.

"You *are* thirteen?"

The girl knew she must stare straight back into the woman's eyes.

"Why aren't you in school?"

For the second time the girl's eyes faltered.

Suddenly Mrs. Hallet knew she had her weapon. Her silence, her eyes demanded an answer. When Rynn spoke her voice was scarcely a whisper.

"Thirteen means I have no rights?"

"Thirteen means you should be in school."

The bewildered girl tried to turn away.

"Look at me when I talk to you!"

"I study at home."

"The school board will see about that. Right now you will take that side of the table."

At Mrs. Hallet's command Rynn thrust her hands into her Levis.

"It so happens *I* am chairman of the school board."

"And every child must do as you say?"

"Every child belongs in school." Furniture *belonged* in its place, children *belonged* in school. Everything, everyone in Mrs. Hallet's well-ordered world had a place.

"School interferes with my education."

"Your father taught you to say that?" When Rynn said nothing, Mrs. Hallet felt she had found the truth.

"Very clever I'm sure. Between you and your father I'm sure you have any number of clever, biting things to say. I can very well imagine the free and easy life you two lived in London. Oh, yes. But *if* you want to live here . . ." By stressing the one word *if*, Mrs. Hallet was able to cast the entire future into doubt. "*Here* you'd do well to remember that some of us who have been in the village a good deal longer than you take pride in carrying out our responsibilities—in knowing how to be good neighbors. If we have to, I can assure you, we also know how to make newcomers feel a good deal less than welcome."

Mrs. Hallet drew the cigarette box from her pocket, found it empty, and hurled the crushed box into the fire.

"No more nonsense out of you. Where is your father?"

"I told you. New York."

"Exactly *where* in New York?" Mrs. Hallet's tone had the mocking edge of a lawyer tearing into a witness during cross-examination.

"He's having lunch with his publisher."

"I want the publisher's telephone number."

"I don't have it."

"Very well, the publisher's name."

Mrs. Hallet grabbed the book from the mantelpiece, tore it open looking for the publisher's name. The book, an English edition, showed a London address, and she shut it with a snap and tossed it back onto the shelf, in disgust as if sensing she had exhausted most of her weapons against the child.

"Your father will call me the minute he comes home. Is that understood?"

Was it a trick of the light? Were tears shining in the little girl's eyes?

"Speak up," snapped the woman, "so I know you understand!"

Rynn was pale but her voice steady, "This is my house."

Mrs. Hallet seized her wicker basket from the table and hurried out the door.

Rynn moved to the corner of the parlor where Gordon stirred in the shadows. Lifting the tiny creature out of his cage, she sat and murmured to him.

4

RYNN HAD PLANNED to go into town during the coming week, but Mrs. Hallet's threat to bring the girl's truancy before the school board was a worry which, during the night, had grown till she had lain wide awake shaking with terror. She decided it would be safer to do her errands when other girls and boys were on the streets. On Saturday no one would question why a thirteen-year-old girl was not in school.

On Saturdays and Sundays she was free to come and go as she chose.

At the bus stop across the street from a house with an iron deer on the lawn Rynn stood alone, a steady rain drumming on the huge black umbrella her father had brought from London. Under its shelter, bundled in her moss-green duffle coat and high rubber boots, she was warm and dry.

A yellow bus, that sent water splashing as it squealed to a stop, banged open its doors and swallowed up the girl among the passengers making the windows dim with their warmth.

The bus was not full, but she felt uncomfortable,

crowded, among these people and hurried past them to sit alone in the long seat at the back.

Car headlights glowed in the rainy afternoon and multicolored neon signs flashed across the mist of the windows.

She felt stifled, for she found the air in the bus, like the air in most public places in America, unbearably hot, and she unbuttoned her duffle coat. From her pocket she pulled a paperback book of poems by Emily Dickinson. She studied the drawing on the cover, the young woman in the severe black dress, the dark hair parted in the middle, the grave, infinitely wise face with its enormous eyes. In many ways, but for the eyes, Rynn felt she and Emily Dickinson looked remarkably alike—Rynn and this woman now dead for ninety years, who in the words of another poet, "eavesdropped on the world."

She held the book, turning the cover to study the face from another angle.

Yes, she was certain, they *did* look alike.

Her father had said so.

She began to read.

> That Love is all there is,
> Is all we know of Love;

In seats facing the aisle in front of her, two girls shrieked with laughter. They carried sticks with felt pennants bright with snarling cat faces and WILDCATS blazoned on the cloth. The two friends talked in loud voices for the benefit of the girl who pretended to read. All of it was about boys and "The Game," and Rynn assumed what they meant by that was American football. Huddled together over their secrets, they were giggling, whispering, and bursting—every few seconds—into new shrieks of laughter.

Once Rynn met the eyes of the girl with glasses.

Rynn found herself wishing her eyes were as large as the girl's, although she told herself the glasses undoubtedly magnified their size. When the girl laughed and briefly showed braces on her teeth, Rynn's envy vanished. The other girl had a muddy complexion and nothing to envy but a red wool coat of a color that reminded Rynn of the Queen's horse guards.

The two stole glances at the girl who sat by herself, and the girl with the glasses and the braces, making no effort to conceal a whisper, turned to her friend who was preparing to blow a pink bubble from pouting lips. The girl with the growing bubble listened and then almost strangled on her gum as she nodded, burying giggles against her friend's white wool scarf.

Rynn told herself if this was what having a friend meant it was a waste of time. It was silly.

The mouth with braces again whispered to her friend, and both girls yelped with laughter.

Rynn knew they were talking about her, and she felt her cheeks and forehead go hot.

Slowly she turned a page, showing deep concentration on her book, yet after a moment of pretending to read, she found a poem so beautiful that she shut her eyes and thought of the quiet New England village where Emily Dickinson had lived and died. Her village, Rynn thought, probably wasn't all that different from the one she lived in —giant elms, quiet streets, small wooden houses, an ancient graveyard. Snow in the winter, lawns with long shadows in the summer.

Emily Dickinson, one could be certain, didn't have silly friends. She didn't need them.

A pink bubble of gum swelled till at last it burst, and the girl who blew it lapped its pink remains back into her mouth, unperturbed. Eyes streaming with laughter, they wiped their tears with a shared wad of Kleenex. Suddenly they screamed and tugged violently on the cord signaling the bus to stop.

They fled out the back door in a final burst of giggles crying:

"Yeah Wildcats!"

On the seat they left behind a thin magazine which Rynn picked up. A boy in vivid colors on the cover smiled at her. His was the face of an exceedingly pretty English lady one might see in a posh shop in Knightsbridge or standing knee deep in heather in a perfume advertisement. She studied the boy. His eyes were huge (she wished hers were as big), his complexion flawless, and his hair long and soft enough to be the envy of any girl. Beneath his picture bold print announced that the lady-faced boy's latest record album had shattered all sales records. Rynn, turning the pages, found photographs of the singing star swarmed by girls of her age, open-mouthed, gazing lovesick at this slender boy who forever smiled and most often clutched a guitar. WHY—the headline of the story demanded—DO THEY TELL US WE'RE TOO YOUNG TO LOVE?

"Why, indeed," Rynn said with an exaggerated yawn as she tossed the thin magazine back on the aisle seat and rode the rest of the way into town with Emily Dickinson.

First on her list of errands was the bank.

Her father had chosen a bank that was open on Saturday mornings, and because of the heavy rain she was surprised to see so many people—entire families in bright-colored coats and scarves and muddy boots. Even dogs trotted into the bank, including a Dalmatian who expressed his happiness by barking and lashing his white tail against her.

She was the only one at the safe deposit desk, and a tap on the little push bell brought a clerk, a tall girl who wore a thick makeup, almost a spun-sugar pink, which failed to cover a deeply-pitted complexion. The little girl had already written her signature and the box number on a slip of paper which the clerk used in a search for a file card.

"Jacobs, Leslie A.?" the girl asked in a flat voice. She stared at the little girl.

"And Rynn. R-Y-N-N. That's my signature there. It's what you call, here in America, a joint account."

The clerk compared the signatures. "You got your key?"

The little girl held up a silver key which she had taken from a chain around her neck. The clerk pressed a button and the lock on the door beside the desk buzzed like a bumble bee Rynn had once caught in a glass jar.

In a room flashing with fluorescent light, the clerk opened a shiny steel door and stepped aside to let Rynn draw a black box from the wall.

"Now you take it into one of those rooms," the clerk said, indicating a row of booths.

"Yes, I know."

A few minutes later, when Rynn returned the black box to the wall inside the safe and the clerk had locked the door and returned the key, a junior officer, a young man with sideburns and yellow teeth, joined the clerk to watch the little girl leave the safe deposit department and cross the shiny marble floor to join a line at a window.

"Isn't she awfully young?" said the yellow teeth.

"Seems to know what she's doing," said the clerk with the pink makeup.

Rynn wrote her name on two twenty-dollar traveler's checks. A young teller, who was attempting, unsuccessfully, to grow a moustache, frowned as he studied the signatures. He looked at the little girl, then at the two checks.

Rynn felt her heart pounding. Why was he doing this?

They were her checks. She had every right to cash her own checks.

"These are yours?" The teller's thin moustache barely moved as he talked.

"Why don't you call an officer of the bank?" she asked rather sharply.

The man glanced around, but if he was looking for someone to authorize the transaction, he found no one. He slid a piece of blank paper across the counter at her.

"Sign your name again. On this."

Didn't anyone ever say *please?*

Without a word the little girl wrote her name in the same careful handwriting that appeared on the check.

The teller waved at a plump woman with several loops of clacking beads swinging around her neck. The beads clattered on the counter as she joined the teller in studying the signature. She shot a doubtful look at the girl.

"Do you have any identification?"

From her duffle-coat pocket, where she carried her wallet, Rynn drew out a British passport.

The teller opened the document and held it in front of the plump woman.

"She's only thirteen."

The plump woman untangled glasses that hung among her beads to inspect the girl who was only thirteen years old.

"You traveling with your mother and father?"

"My father has an account here."

The Dalmatian bounded past Rynn, his tail lashing her legs.

"Jacobs. Leslie A.," the girl said.

The plump woman gave her another long look.

"It's okay," she said.

Apparently it was not okay with the teller, who showed

increasing annoyance when Rynn asked for her money in one-dollar bills. Finishing the transaction, he motioned for the little girl to move on to count her money. Others, he said, were waiting in the line behind her.

But she did not move. "May I have the paper with my signature, please?"

The thin moustache contracted in annoyance as the young man pushed the paper across the counter. As she walked away, Rynn tore the paper into bits and dropped it in a waste paper basket.

So many people on the street. So much hurrying, so many packages.

Rynn's second errand, a plumbing supply store, was several streets away in a quieter part of town where she found herself the only person in the shop. She wandered around looking at the models of heaters, diagrams of central heating systems, and cutaway displays of airducts that kept Americans so hot. A large advertisement that stated that winter was the wise time to air-condition your house urged a refrigerated summer. After minutes alone in the reception area she wondered if anyone was in the warehouse in the back of the counter.

"Hello?" Silence. She called again.

An unusually cheery man, very old and turning up the amplification on his hearing aid, hurried to the counter munching a bologna sandwich. "Morning," he said, gulping down a large chunk of sandwich. "What can we do for you?"

"My name's Jacobs. My father and I have the Wilson house—in the lane."

"Here in town?"

"The village."

The man nodded and took another crescent-shaped bite from the sandwich.

"Our wall heater you put in for the Wilsons has a label that says it came from this shop."

The man nodded. He knew the Wilsons.

"Trouble?" He carefully placed the rest of his sandwich down on a piece of office stationery.

Rynn explained that she did not know if she had trouble or not, but when she had been housecleaning the other day she had read on the dial that at night one turns the dial all the way down to a setting marked NIGHT.

"That's right." The man smiled. "But why don't you let your mother and father worry about that?"

"Shouldn't I?"

With another smile the man shrugged. "Like I said, what can we do for you?"

"When one turns the dial all the way down, there's still a flame that keeps burning. Quite high actually."

"Pilot light."

"Is that perfectly safe? After all, it *is* gas and gas *can* be dangerous." As if this were an accusation she felt demanded proof, she found herself adding, "I mean in London, one of our neighbors was found dead because something had gone wrong with the gas."

"Haven't got a thing to worry about." The man's words were muffled by his mouthful of sandwich. He came around the counter and led the girl to a model: It was the same as the wall heater at Rynn's home.

"Show you why." He pried the cover off the heater and explained how the pilot light, the little blue flame, fired the burner. More important he showed the girl how the gas was fed through one little copper tube. From the burner an air vent opened through the wall of the house to the outdoors.

"See?" he asked with a smile that included a considerable portion of unswallowed sandwich.

"Yes I do," the girl said in her rather crisp way. "And I

do feel ever so much better about it." She turned to the door.
"Thank you very much indeed."

The man was still smiling and munching as Rynn left,
and she imagined that very likely he thought it strange that
a girl of thirteen would come into his shop to ask a question about one of his heaters. Why? Should little girls *not*
be interested in things like that?

She had saved her next errand till last, because it was
what she most wanted to do. Even now, on the street in
front of a bookstore, studying the shiny jackets of masses of
books on display as eagerly as a starving urchin might stare
into a bakery window, she was postponing the ultimate
happiness, the moment when she would actually set foot
inside the bookshop. Then she would be in a world she felt
was far more wonderful than Alice found down the rabbit
hole or the astronauts discovered out in the black vastness
of space.

Once inside the shop, surrounded by tables of books,
shelves of books, stacks of books, she repeated the process
of postponing what she wanted most—the magic moment
she stood before the shelves crowded with thin volumes
of poetry.

Two hours later she still sat on the floor devouring page
after page in books whose bindings cracked with newness
each time her careful hands turned back the cover. Of the
shoppers above her moving through the aisle, she was
oblivious.

No one bothered her. No clerk asked to be of help or
suggested that she move on. But a moment came when her
throat was choked with so much emotion and her face felt
so hot with excitement that she ran from the bookshop into
the cold street.

She spent another hour in a record shop surrounded by
sound and imagining the joy of carrying away armloads

of albums. As she left the bins of classical records and trailed slowly toward the door, she saw the boy on the magazine cover. From a poster his enormous eyes stared down at her, his dazzlingly white grin held her for a long moment.

At a counter stool in Woolworth's, Rynn gave up trying to eat a greasy hamburger. She forced down an orange drink, flat and flavorless, which a black girl had brought after considerable confusion when Rynn had asked for an orange squash. The black girl kept looking at the English girl and the English girl kept drinking.

On the street, waiting for the bus, she tried not to think about what she must do next, for that thought filled her with dread.

She stayed on the bus all the way to the village square with its cannon from the Revolutionary War and pyramid of cannon balls. Leaving the bus she forced herself to hurry under the bare branches of the elms toward a red-brick building with white columns, the town hall.

The front door was open, but inside the halls and offices were as silent as Rynn had hoped they would be at this time on a Saturday afternoon. The silence was so complete, she wondered if she would find anyone to complete her errand, anyone to answer her question.

As she walked down the hall she heard a typewriter tapping. Someone *was* here.

At footsteps, she turned. A tall woman in a raincoat, her hair under a scarf, was hurrying down the corridor toward her. The woman stopped. Her face looked very English. Hair that tumbled from the scarf was gray. Rynn was certain the woman was English, but when she spoke she was unmistakably American.

"What are you doing here?"

Rynn told herself the woman had no right to challenge

her this way. And yet she found herself searching desperately for an explanation.

Before she could speak the woman demanded: "Why aren't you at the game?"

Why indeed? Rynn knew she would have to answer, and though she now saw there was nothing but kindness in the woman's smiling face, and certainly her question, once it was understood, was not a challenge but nothing more than a pleasantry, still—it did require an answer.

"Do you work here?" she asked.

"Not exactly," the woman said with a smile. "I try to help out on some of the committees."

"I'm doing a paper on government," Rynn said. "I need to know when the school board holds its meetings."

"Would it help to visit one?" the woman asked.

"Actually, all I really need to know is when the board meets."

"Twice a month, the second and last Thursday. Eleven o'clock. They met this week. The next won't be for another two weeks . . ." She stopped. "No, that's Thanksgiving so it's canceled."

The woman thought for a bit.

"I can get you the bylaws; would that help?"

She went into an office and returned with a brochure. "This is rather complete, but if you find you need any more help . . ."

"It's fine," Rynn said. "Thank you very much."

"But you shouldn't be working now. You should be at the football game. The Wildcats need all the help they can get."

The girl nodded.

"Whose class are you doing the paper for?"

Suddenly Rynn's green eyes lit up. "Excuse me," she said with a kind of excitement which she seldom showed to

others, "do you *really* think it would be all right if I went
to the game?"

The woman glanced at her watch. "If you hurry you'll
get there by half time."

Rynn turned and ran down the hall. Still smiling, the
woman walked toward the sound of the typewriter's tapping.

Rynn ran all the way home in the rain.

"The school board doesn't meet for another two weeks!
And even then it's canceled!" She laughed and her breath
came out in a mist. "Mrs. Hallet, you're a liar!" She laughed
aloud. "A liar is what you are Mrs. Hallet! *Liar! Liar!*"

She burst into her little house to reach the telephone
book where she searched for a number. As she dialed she
looked across the room to a cardboard carton full of jelly
glasses that stood on the gateleg table.

As she waited for an answer to her call, she listened to the
rain drumming on the roof.

"Mr. Hallet? This is Rynn Jacobs. Fine, yes—is your
mother there? I see. She wanted some jelly glasses I wasn't
able to get for her yesterday. If you'd tell her I have them
ready anytime she wants to come round. Yes, I'll be
here. . . ."

Suddenly the girl's voice was surprisingly cold. "No. It
would be better if *she* came. You see, Mr. Hallet, my father
may have something he wants to talk with her about. Thank
you, Mr. Hallet."

5

A SHARP KNOCK brought Rynn to the hall. Still excited by the discovery of Mrs. Hallet's lie, she flung the door open to find not the woman, but an unexpected caller. She stifled a gasp, for the man standing in the rain was enormous, a giant looming large at the door of a doll's house. He said his name was Police Officer Ron Miglioriti.

The girl said her name was Rynn Jacobs and after that said nothing.

She had no fear of policemen. In England she never knew these young men to be anything but polite, unfailingly friendly and helpful: She never saw them in any activity but strolling, almost ambling along the sidewalks as if the only emergency they might face was to help the next old lady find the location of a street or a bus stop. In America, Rynn had never met an officer, but she had no reason to believe them any different. This one stood before her, his glistening rain slicker streaming water. Something absurdly like those plastic covers she snapped over dishes before putting leftovers in the refrigerator covered his policeman's cap. He had blue-black sideburns and heavy black eye-

brows that almost met over shining black eyes. His nose
had a rather odd look as if it might have been broken, but
every one of his teeth was perfect and his smile was posi-
tively radiant, full of enough morning sunshine to light up
the doorway even on this gray day. Looking at him standing on her porch in the rain after he asked to see her father,
Rynn felt she had no choice but to let him come into her
house.

She was grateful that before he came in, the officer shook
his cape of rainwater. Once inside, he tried not to drip on
her freshly waxed floor.

To her surprise she offered the man a cup of tea.

In the kitchen she reminded herself that even if he
seemed likable, his smile had nothing to do with the reason
that brought him here.

What did he want?

She had a terrifying thought. Had Mrs. Hallet sent him?
But Rynn knew the school board had not met. That was not
the reason. Was he here to pick up the jelly glasses? She
decided whatever the reason it would be better to relax, and
it was the officer's name which made this possible. At first
she found it difficult, but now it struck her as having poetic
possibilities. By the time she poured the tea Rynn was pro-
nouncing it with a nice, rolling Italian accent.

"Miglioriti."

The officer smiled, his usual response, it seemed, to everything. But over the teacup his heavy brows drew together
and met in a frown. He was finding it difficult if not impossible to get his huge thumb and forefinger around the
teacup's handle. The cup wobbled.

Rynn stared at his hand. Large, square and strong. She
imagined on other Saturdays not many years before, this
same hand held a football. Football would explain the
broken nose.

Still frowning, Miglioriti juggled the cup and managed a sip of tea.

"Has your family been in the village long?" She used tea-party manners when she spoke.

A grin spread slowly across Miglioriti's face.

"Sounds like you've been talking with Mrs. Hallet."

Mrs. Hallet. Did she send him?

Officer Miglioriti managed another sip of tea before he spoke.

"Don't tell her I said it, but according to Mrs. Hallet, you have to smell of whale oil off the first sailing ship that ever put in here or to her you'll always be an immigrant."

"I suppose we're the newest," Rynn quickly added, "my father and I."

"At least Mrs. Hallet let you in the village. She doesn't let in everybody. Not if she can help it." Miglioriti attempted a third sip but splashed tea into the saucer. He looked around the sitting room. "She must have approved of you enough to lease you this house."

Rynn took her tea with a precision she believed the policeman considered very British.

"I expect," she said, "she let us in because my father's a poet. That's one of his books. There, on the mantelpiece."

Miglioriti was happy to put his jiggling teacup on the mantel. He reached inside his wet raincape and carefully dried his big hands on a handkerchief before he picked up the thin book.

"He wrote this?" he asked with considerable awe.

Rynn watched him over her teacup. He was like a huge black bear examining a flower. He turned the pages slowly, clearly impressed.

"I'm sorry my father's translating right now. When he's in his study translating and that door's shut, I'm under the strictest orders to see that no matter what happens, he's not disturbed."

The giant's hands turned the pages one at a time.

"Would you like him to sign a copy for you?"

The officer's face broke into another of his radiant smiles.

"Sure—that is if he can spare one."

She liked everything about the man, even the absurd rain cover on his hat. She loved the way he held the book: He made it clear he had respect; he realized it was something precious.

"First author I ever knew."

Rynn sipped tea. "He'll be happy to hear we've gotten to know one another. My father says it's always a very good idea to get to know the local constabulary."

"I know this must be great poetry, but don't laugh if I tell you something?"

"I won't laugh."

"Well I can never really believe people like poetry. I'm not counting birthday card stuff, but, you know—poetry. Stuff that doesn't even rhyme."

Rynn forgot her chipped tooth and smiled in acknowledgment of that wonderful moment when near strangers find they share something more than mutual agreement, when they both reach a point of shared intuition. When she remembered her tooth she covered her smile.

"I'm not laughing at you," she said. "I used to ask him the same thing. Most people like poetry to rhyme."

"I guess I'm like most people then."

"No. You're honest. My father says most people who say they like poetry only pretend to like it."

"I guess you like it?"

"I love it very much." Her long hair swirled as she shook her head to correct herself. "That's redundant. The word 'love' stands alone. 'Very much' only weakens it. I love words. Most people aren't very careful with them."

"You should try listening to witnesses some time. Simplest kind of statement and you can count on them to get it all messed up every time."

If Mrs. Hallet had sent this officer *why was he waiting to tell her what she wanted?*

"He must be good—your father."

"T. S. Eliot said he was. My father knew Sylvia Plath when she was married to Ted Hughes. Of all living English poets, Hughes is my favorite. He likes Emily Dickinson, too. She's my favorite of all."

Rynn shut her eyes.

She began to speak. Her voice was unlike all the teachers Miglioriti had ever heard intone poetry in school—natural, clear, and not a bit affected. She was not trying to force her own meaning to the words; she was letting the words say what they had to say.

> There's a certain Slant of light,
> Winter Afternoons—
> That oppresses, like the Heft
> Of Cathedral Tunes—
>
> Heavenly Hurt, it gives us—
> We can find no scar,
> But internal difference,
> Where the Meanings, are—
>
> None may teach it—Any—
> 'Tis the Seal Despair—
> An imperial affliction
> Sent us of the Air—

> When it comes, the Landscape listens—
> Shadows—hold their breath—
> When it goes, 'tis like the Distance
> On the look of Death—

The maple log in the fireplace burned through and fell with a tiny crash of sparks. Rynn lifted the woodbox lid, took out the poker, and pushed the broken log into a mass of red coals.

"Do you love that too?"

"'Shadows hold their breath,' . . . I sure like that."

She smiled at him without opening her mouth.

Miglioriti put the book back on the fireplace mantel. "Sounds especially good—the way you say it."

"I love the way it sounds. Like I love 'Miglioriti.'"

The young man blushed. Strange. Her father always said it was impossible to embarrass an Italian.

"Like I said, I've never known a poet."

"Neither has Mrs. Hallet. I think it thrills her quite a bit."

"You've been here since September?"

"Ever since we saw the yard blazing with zinnia. Red and gold and purple and white and orange. . . . First we saw the zinnias. Then I heard the ocean. And the trees. Did you know they talk?"

"That's more than some of the people here do."

Rynn grinned to show she got his joke.

His smile was wide. "I guess, then, you could say, you like it here?"

"I love it."

"School okay?"

Rynn swallowed, forcing down the panic that rose within her. She shrugged. "It's okay."

"Being new isn't easy. People around here can seem a little cold at first."

"That's okay too. . . ."

"After you've been here longer," the man was smiling to show he was still joking, "they get even colder."

Rynn forgot her tooth and laughed. When she found the big man watching her closely, she quickly closed her mouth.

"You're quite funny. For a policeman."

He asked whether she meant funny peculiar or funny ha-ha. She said he was the most ha-ha cop she had ever met.

"Most American cops don't drink tea, either. Ever notice?"

He was looking around the room. "This used to be the Wilsons' place."

"And you're going to tell me it's haunted?"

"Not a chance. Happiest people you could ever meet."

"Until." The girl held up a warning finger and spoke in a dark tone appropriate for a ghost story. "*Until* they met grotesque, mysterious, and quite extraordinarily hideous deaths."

"No. As a matter of fact they inherited a couple of million dollars and live on the French Riviera."

"Good! I knew it was a lucky house!" She looked at the man in the shiny raincape who stood on the hearth.

"I like knowing you're our policeman."

"Thanks." Miglioriti's grin was almost boyish. "Sure beats being called a 'pig.' I mean how would you like being called a pig? These days kids don't have any respect for the law."

Rynn wished she could ask him to take the absurd refrigerator cover from his hat and shed his rain slicker. But now that he had finished his tea she dared not encourage him to stay. She reminded herself not to like this man too much. His presence here raised a question that was still unanswered.

Miglioriti picked up his saucer and teacup. "All in all, the village is a pretty good place to live. Just don't let Mrs.

Hallet hassle you. She'll try to. Like I said, she thinks she runs the place."

"Does she?"

"Parts of it I wish she would."

"Meaning?" With a boldness that surprised her Rynn looked directly at the police officer, a look that demanded an answer.

"That's all." He had said too much, and now he wanted to avoid going any further. He picked up his cup and saucer.

"Meaning her son?"

"You met him already?"

Rynn spoke very quietly, but this time it was without looking at the officer.

"He says I'm a very pretty girl."

"You are." The man was choosing his words carefully. "But it might sound better coming from someone your own age."

"Is he a deviate?"

Miglioriti looked around for a place to put the cup and saucer.

"What do I do with this?"

Rynn took the delicate china from his big hand.

"He has two children," she said.

"Yeah," the officer said, clearly unconvinced.

She recalled feeling how unlike a father the man with the pink hands and face had seemed as he stood in this very room. Again she surprised herself with her boldness.

"Are they really his?"

For a moment she did not think Miglioriti was going to answer. When he did he seemed to be speaking to a grown person, someone who could be expected to understand the full implication of what he was saying. "His wife's. From another marriage."

"In other words"—the girl dared to look at the officer—

"Mr. Hallet is the kind of man who tries to give candy to little girls?"

Miglioriti pulled off his cap and ran his big square fingers through his dark mass of curly hair. He did not choose to answer. He shook his head in feigned incomprehension.

"Where did you say you came from?"

"London mostly."

"I guess kids grow up fast in big towns."

She finished her tea and put it with the officer's cup and saucer on the kitchen counter. "My father and I've lived in a lot of places. We've known all kinds of people." She carried the tea things to the sink. She was looking out the window over the kitchen sink into the back garden, rank with overgrown weeds and dead flowers.

"Why isn't Mr. Hallet under treatment?"

"Like what did you have in mind?"

She realized the officer was letting her do most of the talking. "There's such a thing as psychoanalysis."

Now it was Miglioriti's turn to talk and it would be difficult not to say more than he intended, for the two were still sharing the unusual intimacy of a shared intuition.

"Two places people who've been out here on the Island for three hundred years don't go. They don't go to psychoanalysts, and they don't go to jail."

Rynn was running tap water onto the dishes. "You have my solemn word I shan't take any candy from strangers." She turned off the water, dried her hands and returned to the officer.

"I'm glad you came by."

"Except I haven't told you why I came."

Rynn hoped she had not shown the sense of cold shock she felt. She fought to keep her eyes looking straight into his.

She waited for him to speak.

"You like turkey?"

"I'm supposed to say yes?"

"You don't."

"If you want the truth, no. Not very much." Immediately she felt she should give this pleasant man a reason. "Birds are reptiles. Way back, biologically. Did you know that?"

"I guess I didn't." He put on his shower-cap police officer's hat. "Then you won't want any raffle tickets?"

"You mean if my father and I buy tickets we might win a turkey?"

"Chances are you won't win." He seemed very earnest about the raffle. "For Thanksgiving. Twenty-five pound minimum. Course that is a lot of turkey if you don't like turkey." He was moving to the door. He grinned. "Your father like turkey?"

"Even less than I do. We'll take two tickets."

"Wow," the young officer said, taking his cap off and plowing his fingers through his shiny black hair. "I really hate doing this, you know? I'd a lot rather be at the football game this afternoon. Doing this I always sort of feel I'm blackmailing people."

"Not at all," Rynn said in her most worldly manner. "It's for a worthy cause. At home in England you'd be surprised the things the Queen has to sell tickets for."

Miglioriti looked at the girl. She looked at him, and her grin was wide enough, for a second, to show her broken tooth.

"How much are they?"

"For two? Two dollars."

"Just a second."

Rynn made a sign that the officer was not to leave, and she ran up the stairs to the second floor, which was above the closed door of the study.

Miglioriti, finding himself alone in the parlor, hurried

to the hall and the study door and knocked softly. There was no answer. He tried the knob, but the door was locked. From the top of the stairs came the little girl's voice.

"One. Two dollars." She took the stairs two at a time unfolding bills as Miglioriti drew a book of tickets from his pocket and tore the tickets from the stub.

"And if my father and I are *very* unlucky," Rynn said with a smile, "we win a twenty-five pound turkey?"

They both laughed.

Miglioriti beamed. "Why is it English kids are always so polite? Never catch *them* calling us 'pigs.'" Rynn folded the lottery tickets. The officer was still smiling. "I wish we had more like you around here. Sure would make my job easier." He put the book of tickets inside his jacket. "Well, I guess I better go hustle more turkey tickets. Thanks for the tea. *And* the sympathy."

The little girl and the policeman shared grins.

"Thank your father, too."

"I will." She crossed to the door with him. "Shall we see you again?"

"Can't avoid me. We get to be a pretty small place in the winter." He opened the door.

"Still raining."

"Like home."

Miglioriti took off his hat and made sure the plastic liner was snapped into place. He pulled the cap back down over his black hair and went out.

From under the dripping wet trees the officer called back to the girl, "Thanks again, Miss Jacobs. And I hope you don't win the turkey."

Watching the dark young man go, Rynn felt a sudden loss. She was still looking into the misty afternoon even after the patrol car left the lane.

For a long time she breathed the cold air that was heavy

with the smell of wet leaves and thought of days like this in London's Hyde Park when the naked trees looked like black-and-white pen drawings in a children's book.

Another car came down the lane, a dark-red car that stopped before the house. A metal door slammed and the woman in a tweed coat hurried toward her under a bright-red candy-stripe umbrella.

Rynn waited till the woman in the scratchy coat had almost reached the door.

"Hello, Mrs. Hallet."

The woman lowered her umbrella. Her hard blue eyes narrowed in fat pouches at the sight of the girl already at the entrance. Her voice was cold.

"I *may* come in?"

"I invited you."

6

RYNN GRIPPED the door handle as Mrs. Hallet's squelching shoes printed mud with every step across the polished oak floor. By striding through the house and stationing herself in front of the fire, Mrs. Hallet was making her declaration—any rights the child had claimed during their last visit were now dismissed.

The woman tapped the umbrella's steel tip on the hearthstones to shake off the rainwater. She snapped the candy stripes open and shut to shed more drops into the fireplace.

"Never open an umbrella inside the house." The girl remembered the words of a neighbor in London, an old woman with no teeth who lived entirely on condensed milk and who, one rainy day like today, had shrieked that warning at her. Of all the kinds of bad luck one could bring on, the woman had warned, opening an umbrella inside the house brought the very worst. Rynn remembered the warning, but prided herself on her own lack of superstition. Mrs. Hallet, she found herself forced to admit, did not look like the kind of woman on whom bad luck would dare thrust itself.

Leaving the door wide open to the rain, to show the woman at the fireplace that she did not expect her to stay in the house any longer than it took to pick up the jelly glasses, Rynn moved into the parlor, yanked the curtains shut and switched on a lamp. Making the room ready for the night had been an impulse, an instinct. The woman could not escape the change. The girl had made the house seem smaller, cosier, more than ever her own place.

Rain beat on the roof and splashed outside the door.

Rynn knew Mrs. Hallet was waiting for her full attention before she spoke. She also knew this woman, in shadow against the fire's glow, was carefully considering what she was about to say. Neither seemed prepared when the woman's voice cracked out—sharp as the breaking of a dry tree branch.

"This morning I spoke to the school board about you."

This was enough to begin. She had let Rynn know, even if this were the girl's home, that it was a child to whom she was talking.

Rynn had vowed not to challenge her, but in her anger at this invasion she had to fight to keep from screaming into the pink face that she knew this was a lie, a stupid lie, that anyone—any child of intelligence—could expose simply by learning when the board held its meetings.

Rynn said nothing.

How often she was amazed at the lies adults told. Silly, easy-to-expose lies. Did they not remember how difficult it is to deceive a child? Had they forgotten that when it comes to lying children know all there is to know?

The silence seemed endless, but only a few seconds had passed. The woman could not resist flicking hard blue eyes toward the girl to determine the impact of her opening attack.

"When they learned about your case, I must say, they were very interested."

"You're a liar, Mrs. Hallet. A liar!" Rynn screamed to herself. Instead, she said, "I was just about to put the kettle on. Would you care for a cup of tea?" Her voice was as pleasant, as unchallenging as she could manage.

But Mrs. Hallet had no intention of allowing Rynn to blunt her attack with good manners.

"Very interested indeed."

How Rynn fought to scream "Liar!" at her. How she ached to shout into that fat, pink face that she knew the school board had met last Thursday, that she knew it would not meet for another month. She longed to tell this lying old woman that, by the time she had to face the reality and not merely these threats, she was bright enough, clever enough, bold enough to think of some way to stay out of their school. She *would* escape them. She would *never* play their game.

"You don't want to know what they said?"

"For tea I can offer you Earl Grey's or Darjeeling."

The woman snapped the umbrella shut, glaring at this child who stared so directly at her with a face that was neither innocent nor sweet, nor openly challenging. Her eyes, searching Rynn's impassive face, wavered, and in that fleeting instant, before she could regain her steady gaze, betrayed her uncertainty. Had this child caught her in a lie? It was stupid to lie about the meeting, something the girl could so easily check. Nonsense. This was just a child. Nevertheless she retreated to her strongest weapon—the full force of her years.

"I came here quite prepared to forget what happened yesterday. However, I must say, I don't care for your tone any better today."

"Then it's up to me to apologize." Rynn realized that in

London she had never sounded this English. "If I've offended you in any way, Mrs. Hallet, I *am* sorry."

But, of course, she knew very well that an apology was
not what the woman wanted. Just as she knew it was not
the jelly glasses that had brought her here.

Mrs. Hallet twisted the red, candy-striped folds tight
against the umbrella rod.

"What I find particularly surprising is that most English
boys and girls are so well behaved." This kind of hauteur
called for her coldest look, a look to turn a child to stone, and
if not stone, at the very least, tears.

She found no change in the little girl's face.

"But then, you're not *truly* English are you?"

"What did you decide about the tea?"

"Not a glass of thick, sweet wine you people use in your
religious rituals?"

Rynn's face shining in the firelight, was still a mask.

Mrs. Hallet, the first to break the lock between their eyes,
seized the excuse of the umbrella to cover her defeat and
she moved to the hall to hang its bright stripes on a wooden
peg.

"Or aren't you old enough to drink wine?" she said, preparing her cross-examination. She slammed the door and
strode with muddy steps that brought her brushing past the
girl back into the room.

"You did tell my son fourteen. You told *me* thirteen. Now
which is it to be?"

"Thirteen."

"And brilliant. As so many of your people are."

"Mrs. Hallet, will you please accept my apology for what
happened yesterday?"

The woman waited until she had returned to her posi-
tion of command at the hearth before she spoke.

"Have you learned to say it the way the phonograph

record does?" She stretched her hands to the fire and appeared to consider the apology. "I'm very much afraid it isn't that simple. The more I've thought about what happened here yesterday, the more convinced I've become that you and your father would find yourselves far more at home some place where you could—let's say—speak the language you seem to prefer."

With the poker from the woodbox the woman jabbed the flames. Her metallic hair flashed in the light, as if on fire.

"On the telephone you made a great point to my son that your father wished to speak with me. Here I am. I certainly wish to speak to him. He is home?"

"Yes."

"Call him."

"I'm afraid right now he's translating. He couldn't be disturbed—even for Officer Miglioriti."

"Officer Miglioriti works for people like me," Mrs. Hallet said, making it unmistakable that the girl was never again to confuse power and the law with some affable young man whom she could hire or fire.

"It's high time," she said, "that all of us faced the simple fact that we've made a mistake about this house." The fire blazed.

Mrs. Hallet warmed her hands. "In case you're wondering what I'm doing, I'm waiting right here till you call your father."

"You didn't answer—about the tea."

Mrs. Hallet gave herself a long moment to study the room as if the considerations of the previous day enabled her to see it in a new light.

"The two of you, living here—in this lane—so few neighbors. And with winter coming and so little in common with the rest of us. No. I shouldn't think it would be your sort of place at all. For the life of me I can't imagine what made any of us think you could be happy here—"

"My father and I love this house—"

"Such a lonely place for a little girl who's by herself so much of the time. No. I think we'll make other plans—"

"We have a lease for three years."

Mrs. Hallet continued to rub her pink hands. "Leases have been known to be broken. No. It wouldn't surprise me to learn your father has already decided to go somewhere you'll both feel more comfortable."

"You mustn't worry about us, Mrs. Hallet."

"There it is again. That continual mocking tone. And don't look at me with those eyes so full of hurt and pretend you've been misunderstood. You try to act as if you don't intend things to sound the way you say them. But you and I know very well exactly what you intend."

"There are the glasses, Mrs. Hallet. On the table."

"Am I being dismissed?"

At a loss for words, Rynn listened to the woman's deep breathing.

"Call your father!" Her voice was raw with anger. *"Right this minute!"*

"I told you. He can't be disturbed."

Mrs. Hallet had left the fireplace and was already in the hall reaching for the study door, where she paused as if waiting for the girl's command.

When it came, Rynn had never spoken with more authority:

"Don't open that door!"

"You and I know perfectly well," Mrs. Hallet said, "he isn't there."

Rynn's voice was quiet, calm. "Open that door, Mrs. Hallet, and I shall have to tell my father about your son."

"My son?" Mrs. Hallet's hand dropped from the door knob, her words the snarl of a trapped animal.

"About the other evening. I haven't told my father yet."

Though Rynn could not see Mrs. Hallet in the darkness of the hall, she knew the woman's face was fiery with rage.

"Told your father what?"

"What happened here."

Rynn waited, allowing the silence to indict the woman's son.

"The way he acted. Apparently people in the village know all about him—"

Mrs. Hallet sprang from the shadows.

"Miglioriti! He's a liar!"

"Not Officer Miglioriti, Mrs. Hallet." In contrast to the woman's red, raw hysteria, the girl, almost serene, grew in command.

"What did that goddamn wop tell you?"

"Nothing, Mrs. Hallet."

"Nothing? When he's always hated Frank. Did he tell you that before Frank married her, he had an affair with my son's wife? You wonder why he hates my son?"

"He wasn't even going to tell me your son's children aren't his. I had to ask."

"What else did he say? I demand to know what else he said!"

"Even when I asked about psychiatric treatment for your son, or why the police don't do anything—"

Nothing Mrs. Hallet might have done in this moment would have surprised Rynn. But now it was the livid woman's turn to throttle her rage.

"Why should they do anything?"

"When your son offers candy to little girls—?"

With great viciousness the woman slapped the girl a stinging blow across the face. Her face aflame Rynn ran to the table and shoved the carton of clinking glasses close to the edge.

"Your glasses, Mrs. Hallet."

"You are going to get out of this house!"

"*My* house, Mrs. Hallet." Rynn blinked back hot tears.

"With—or without your father—"

Rynn choked down a sob. "It's true, it is a lonely place out here in the lane. Often I am alone. That doesn't worry me, Mrs. Hallet. If it worries *you*, that's a problem you had better work out with your son!"

"Goddamn you!"

The rain drummed on the roof.

Mrs. Hallet moved to the table and thrust her hand into the carton.

"No seals," she said. "Without the rubber seals the glasses are worthless."

Rynn peered into the box. Her hand searched madly, rattling among the glasses. At last, defeated, she closed the carton lid.

The woman held the girl with her stony eyes. "Right now I want the glasses! And the seals. This time, don't you dare tell me to come back later!"

"You don't need those seals," Rynn cried. "You don't even really want those glasses. . . ."

Mrs. Hallet had made other fast, decisive moves, but none had prepared Rynn for the way the woman grabbed the table to drag it off the braided rug. She clutched wildly at the woman's tweed coat.

"Get out of my house!"

Table legs screeched across the oak floor.

Mrs. Hallet flung back the braided rug to reveal a trapdoor. Clawing at the hasp, she pushed back the bolt.

The girl, shaking with rage, felt helpless to move.

The woman lifted the door to its full height before she

dropped it back over its hinges with a slam against the wall.

Her fury turned to terror. Rynn watched stunned as the woman went to the top of the steps and looked down, pulling her tweed coat around her against the cold.

Rynn broke the paralysis of fear to lunge at the woman, but she was shaking so violently she could not complete the move, and she cried out, a cry full of raw fury, a cry shocking in one so young.

"I'm warning you, Mrs. Hallet!"

Her voice had stopped the woman at the study door, but this time Mrs. Hallet paused only long enough to wind her coat more tightly around her before placing her first footstep with a scrape on the ancient stone.

Rynn trembled above the stairwell, almost in a trance, watching the woman's metallic gold hair and the shoulders of the brown tweed coat sink with each step. On the stairs where she was forced to lower her head to pass under the oak planks of the floor, Mrs. Hallet brought her glasses to her face to peer down into the dark.

Another step, then the sound of scraping feet stopped.

"Oh, my God. . . ." Her voice was a whisper.

Then she screamed.

As if the scream were a signal, Rynn leaped forward and pulled the door from the wall. It fell into place, shutting out the scream from below.

Rynn threw her full weight onto the oak planks and clawed at the wrought-iron hasp, bending it on its hinges.

Thuds pounded on the door.

Pushing the rusty bolt back through the hasp took all the girl's force.

Thuds banged from below as Rynn slowly rose from the planks. Each thud, like one of her own heartbeats, drove her back from the door.

A muffled scream, as if far away, was all but shut out by the heavy oak.

Two more thuds.

Suddenly, as she shrank away from the door something sprang at her from behind, blocking her retreat. Not even daring to gasp, she reached behind her to find the empty chair rocking, creaking wildly back and forth . . . back and forth.

7

THE LITTLE GIRL sat rocking. For how long she had
no idea. Was it hours ago she had run to lock the front door
and yank the curtains further shut so no one could see in?
Was it only minutes?

A log burned through and fell into the fireplace.

Rain pattered on the roof.

She rocked, back and forth, back and forth.

Firelight wavered. The room was growing cold.

She sat as catatonic as one of those pitiable wretches forgotten in some madhouse, locked into herself, left to stare
forever at the peeling plaster on the wall or at a point in
the middle distance. But she was not mad, nor was her mind
a blank. Her mind had never been so clear.

For a long time she tried to picture Mrs. Hallet beneath
the shining oak boards of the trapdoor. There had been
muffled cries, many pounds. For hours, or was it only minutes, Rynn had heard nothing. She wondered. Mrs. Hallet,
down in that cold cellar that smelled of old wet newspapers
and crawled with spiders, was she sitting on the ancient
stone steps? Rynn decided that Mrs. Hallet would stand,
stand and wait. No matter how long.

That is what Rynn, in her rocking chair, was doing. Waiting.

Her hands were cold with an icy sweat that she rubbed against her Levis.

She must keep her mind clear. She could do that. After all, didn't everyone say what a brilliant little girl she was? If that were true, now was the time to prove it, prove it by thinking as she had never been forced to think before. She must think carefully and decide, even more carefully, what to do.

First thing to think about: Did she dare open the trapdoor? Did she dare let Mrs. Hallet out?

She rocked steadily.

Even though it had all happened in an instant, though it was something she would never have been able to dream herself capable of doing, it had been done.

Could it be undone?

Even if Rynn lay on the floor and whispered through the trap and down the stairs that she knew what she had done was a terrible thing, even if she begged the woman for forgiveness, if she implored the woman for her pardon, from her dungeon what could Mrs. Hallet say? Of course, from down there in the dark, there was nothing—absolutely nothing—Mrs. Hallet would not promise. Of course, Mrs. Hallet would vow never, never under any circumstances, to tell what the little girl had done.

Of course that would be a lie.

Mrs. Hallet would never forgive her.

Mrs. Hallet with her great sprawling brick house behind the rows of evergreens and a long sweep of lawn in the village; Mrs. Hallet with her powerful friends; Mrs. Hallet who hired and fired men like Miglioriti—Mrs. Hallet would see, if it took to her dying day, that the little girl was punished. Mrs. Hallet would insist the girl pay the full measure of the law for the terrible, the outrageous, the unforgivable thing that had happened. Full measure and more.

What would that mean? Prison? Yes, certainly. In America—as in England—they sent children to prison, children who had done far less than push old ladies down into cellars and lock the door on them. Mrs. Hallet would march into court with half a dozen lawyers and she would stand before the world and tell the terrible thing that had happened to her. The court would listen to her ordeal and stare in shock. When it came time for the little girl with a lawyer appointed by the court to stand before them and try to explain *why* she had done such a thing, who would believe her? Who could forgive such a child?

"Too bad, Mrs. Hallet, because you're the way you are, I can never lift that door and allow you to climb those stairs. There is now no other way. You *must* stay down there, Mrs. Hallet."

The little girl rocked back and forth, back and forth.

Now the next question. What was going to happen to the woman down there? How long would she stay alive?

Keep thinking.

Would she freeze to death? No, the winter, though wet and cold was not yet so severe that the cellar would be cold enough to freeze. Would she starve? Of course, in time. But how long would it take? Rynn had heard of people who fasted. She had read about people who had lived for days, weeks even, without food. Before the woman starved, she would die of thirst. That would take how long? Three days?

The chair rocked. Back and forth.

Keep thinking.

Three days. Go slow now. *Think.* Suppose it took three days for the woman down there to die. In three days anyone might come to the door. They—"they"?—who were "they"? That didn't matter. *They*—someone—would come to the door. People like Frank Hallet and other adults—*they*. *They*—the ones who never bothered to ask a thirteen-year-old girl if they might come into her house. Anyone who did come in would make footsteps and Mrs. Hallet would pound on the trapdoor. Even with the braided rug back in place, even with the gateleg table covering the rug and the trap, the woman could make herself heard from down there.

Three days.

The little girl suddenly had an answer. She would go away for three days. Lock the door and go away. Who could get inside? With the curtains pulled shut who could see into the room? Then who could Mrs. Hallet signal? For a moment the idea of flight warmed her against the overwhelming cold and fear.

Then she went colder than ever.

Frank Hallet knew his mother was coming here this afternoon. He knew that from the telephone call. He would come and look. Another chill. He could get into the house; the real estate office had a key. . . .

Rynn rubbed her arms against the cold.

Watching the trapdoor every step of the way, she crept from the rocking chair and crawled across to the hearth where she stretched her hands out to the warm red glow.

Eyes sparkling in the firelight, she stared at the door.

She shivered. Never before in this house had she trembled with such a bone-chilling cold.

Perhaps, she thought, she would not be so cold if she turned on the heater.

The heater.

The heater was fueled by gas. In London gas from a heater had killed their neighbor.

"But that was in a tiny, little flat," she told herself. "They found the thick carpet up against the crack under the door. The place was practically airtight. . . ."

She looked at the shining oak of the trapdoor. The cellar underneath was even smaller than that flat in London.

She ran to the kitchen and creeping into the cupboard under the sink, pushed and poked among the boxes of washing powders, plastic bottles of bleach, strong-smelling furniture polish, and waxes till she found what she wanted—a long coil of rubber hose.

She pried the metal from the gas heater as she had seen the man in the shop do and let it fall with a clang.

Exactly as the man had shown, she found the pilot light —a silent, steady, blue flame. She knelt and leaned forward and with a breath—almost like blowing out the candles on her birthday cake—she blew. The flame danced wildly in the dark and was gone.

It took her only a few seconds to detach the gas line from the burner and push the rubber tubing over this little pipe. Carrying the other end of the hose she wormed it down into the crack between the trapdoor and the floorboards.

Down there—would the cellar be airtight?

The door itself was thick oak, solid and without a split or crack. But around the edges was the crack. She would have to pack something around those edges.

Working quickly she tore the newspaper with the crossword puzzle into long strips and with a stick of kindling poked these as wads down between the door and the floorboards. All four sides.

She sat back on her heels and examined her work.

"What if someone comes in and smells gas?" She shook her head answering her own question. "If it's airtight the gas *can't* escape. It'll stay down there till it dissipates—or whatever gas does—"

To make sure no gas could possibly escape into the room, Rynn went around the four sides giving the caulking an extra poke with the stick.

Airtight.

Why use gas? If the cellar was airtight, the woman down there would suffocate.

Rynn studied the trap. She knew the door was sealed, but what she could not know was how long the air down there could last. What if there was the tiniest leak in one of the cellar walls to the outside of the house? It might not be enough to stop the gas from filling the chamber, but it might be enough to sustain life. She could not take that chance.

Back at the heater's vent where the man had shown her how the air was conducted through to the outside wall of the house, she checked and saw there was no way for the gas to escape the pipe and the hose.

Now there was only one thing left to do.

She knelt at the front of the heater and turned the dial past all the numbers for the maximum supply of gas.

8

RYNN SHUT the front door very quietly and locked it behind her. Buttoning her heavy wool duffle coat under her chin she looked through the trees at the sky. Although the world was wet as a gray watercolor, the rain had stopped.

She plunged her hands deep into her pockets. One jingled the door keys against her wallet, the other carefully felt for the small warm presence of Gordon.

The cold made her face tingle and she breathed greedily as if she could not get enough of this moist fresh air that smelled so strongly of earth and leaves. She wandered under dripping trees, her boots popping acorns underfoot with every step. Drops of rain sparkled on the polish of horse chestnuts. Dead zinnias scraped at her coat.

She drew Gordon from her pocket so he could enjoy the cold air. His pink nose quivered.

"Take a deep breath," she said. "Makes you feel washed and clean. . . ."

That is when she saw it. Through the black tree trunks, gleaming wet in the gray afternoon—Mrs. Hallet's dark-red Bentley.

Gordon squeaked.

Rynn's fist was too tightly clenching the rat. At another squeak and a scrabble of tiny claws, she dropped him back into her pocket.

Following an instinct, as if by not looking at the car she could deny its presence, Rynn turned away and ran down the lane.

She glanced back only once. There it was, shining out in the wet lane.

A squirrel rattled elm branches.

Gold leaves drifted past.

She tried to put off thinking about the car and what she must do to get rid of it. Did that have to be today? Had she not done all she could do today?

Yes, she had to get rid of the car. Now. But how?

A mile from home she heard the steady honking of a car horn and the blare of rock music. When the sound grew and a car flashed by the crossroads, she saw young passengers her age hanging out the windows waving Wildcat pennants, screaming their excitement. They had won their game. They were loud and happy and young and together with nothing in the world to worry about.

None of them knew the girl who stood alone on the road spangled with wet leaves, but they waved at her.

Rynn raised her hand as if to wave back, but she stopped.

The honking and music faded away in the wet afternoon.

Minutes later, from high overhead, the faint call of birds made her look up to see a straggling V of geese beating their wings slowly, slowly, flying south.

She felt desolate and terribly alone. Those happy kids in the car. Did they ever feel alone and helpless? Why should they? They had families, they had friends. If one of them was scared to death he always had someone to turn to, to talk with. If one of them had to move a car he could ask a brother or sister or telephone a friend—any one of a number of friends.

Rynn told herself sharply that feeling sorry for herself would solve nothing.

But who could she call?

Only once before had she ever felt as entirely alone in the world. She fought the sting of hot tears, but a great sob was rising in her throat. Suddenly blinded with tears and shaking with sobs, she turned and rushed down the lane for home.

As she dashed through her yard she allowed herself only one look at the car.

Still there, the goddamn liver-colored Bentley gleamed out, shining, glinting in the wet.

In the sitting room the gateleg table stood on the braided rug which covered the trapdoor. Rynn, still in her duffle coat at the kitchen counter, had found a service station number in the telephone book's yellow pages, dialed, and was listening to the voice on the other end with growing exasperation, when she cut in impatiently.

"A neighbor was supposed to drive it," she explained. "My father's really counting on the car being at the station. You know yourself one can never get a taxi when one really needs one. No, that's what I already said, the driver doesn't have to be a mechanic. Anyone at your station who can drive. As soon as he can? Thank you so very much."

She was about to hang up, but at what the man at the service station said next, she froze.

"The keys?"

Rynn's voice betrayed none of her panic.

"They're in the car," she said. "I'll be waiting."

She hung up and stood, still frozen, at the kitchen counter.

It took all her determination to dash through the hall and into the front yard.

The gleaming Bentley was locked. All four doors.

With unwilling steps she returned to the house and carefully locked the front door.

Walking slowly, now leaving her own wet footprints on the floor, she crossed the parlor, drew the curtains tight, turned on a lamp, and stared at the gateleg table and braided rug, running her hand across the shining wood as if she had never seen the table before. With sudden force she grabbed it by the edge and dragged it from the rug, scraping it over the bare floor. She hurled the heavy rug from the trap. Her fingers worked at the hasp till the bolt yielded.

For a long moment the girl knelt without moving, fighting, gathering all the courage she needed to raise the trapdoor.

Again it was only by hurling herself with that sudden force that breaks fear with action that she was able to fling back the door which fell with a bang against the wall.

She drew a deep breath, held it, and hurried down the cold stone steps.

In less than a minute, like a surfacing diver gasping for breath, she ran up the steps clasping keys in her hand. Still gasping, she swept up the newspapers that had packed the door's edges, sending them fluttering down into the cellar.

She was lowering the trap when she heard a tapping on the front door.

Her heart stopped.

Not a pound. Not a bang. A tap.

Working frantically she fixed the hasp and spread the braided rug over the door.

Another tap. The girl stiffened.

"Just a minute!"

She was dragging the table back across the oak floor onto the rug, trying to deaden the scraping sound. As the table moved, the jelly glasses in the carton clinked.

Three insistent *rat-a-tats* on the door.

"Coming!"

Rynn looked at the floor. Were there scrape marks in the wax? She knelt and used the bottom of her duffle coat to polish these away. She stepped back to study the room.

Everything seemed to be back in place.

At the window she peered out between the curtains. Her angle on the front door showed no one.

She was in the hall, her hand already on the lock when she saw Mrs. Hallet's umbrella—bright candy stripes—hanging on a peg.

Whoever was out there tapped again.

Only after she lifted down the umbrella, hurled it behind the couch, and took a final deep breath, did she open the door.

Nothing prepared her for what she saw. Here was a man in a shining black-silk top hat and a black cape, a walking stick in his hand.

"Hi," the figure in black said cheerily.

Speechless, Rynn could only stare. A false moustache hung unevenly where it was coming unstuck from beneath the nose. This was no man. This was a boy. How old was he? Sixteen? It was a boy's face, a small, merry face with very black eyes. Tapping his top hat with his stick, he looked like a happy fox in an animated cartoon she had seen.

The boy flourished his black cape in a stage bow—a magician who has just produced a miracle and now waits for acclaim. He raised his face slowly, his black eyes sparkled, a smile flashed a row of small but very white teeth. The smile was, if anything, too much like that of the boy on the magazine cover. Too sweet for a boy.

"I'm Mario Podesta."

The girl did not answer.

"I'm supposed to drive your father's car to the station."

Rynn's hand stayed on the doorknob. "Why are you dressed up like that?"

The black cape swirled and the walking stick tapped the silk hat. "I"—and he stopped long enough to bring the cape over his shoulder with the pride of a matador—"am a magician!"

Rynn looked at the walking stick. "And this is your magic wand."

"Cane," the boy said. "I'm a cripple."

Rynn made no move to stop him as he limped into the room.

She said, "I guess I should say I'm sorry."

"Why? It's not your fault."

They looked at each other, the girl in the duffle coat and Levis, the boy in shiny black.

"Your moustache is on crooked," she said. But very quickly she added, "I like your cape and hat."

"Yeah?" the boy smiled his beautiful smile. No, the small face was not so much foxlike as elfin. Certainly he was some woodland creature out of mythology. A faun perhaps. Only the dark lines under his eyes saved the face from being too beautiful. The lines were deep, painfully etched, in an otherwise untouched face.

He tapped the floor with his cane. "Saturday afternoon when all my brothers are playing football I'm on my way to put on a magic show. For some rich kid's birthday party."

"Truly? You're a real magician?"

"I'd be some asshole to run around like this if I weren't." Again he flourished his cape. "Sure. Like Houdini. Thurston. Blackstone—"

"Prove it." In her excitement, Rynn smiled and she knew

the boy had seen her chipped tooth. She almost clamped her mouth shut when she spoke, "Do something magic."

"All my stuff's out on my bike." He reached his hand out to her.

What did he want?

"The car keys for Christ's sake."

Rynn found herself jolted into realizing why the boy called Mario was here. Dropping the keys into his hand she said, "Here, Mario the Magician."

The boy limped back to the door. "What I'll do is I'll leave the car at the station. But not with the keys in it. Leave the keys in it, some guy'll rip it off."

He looked at the girl whose green eyes were studying him carefully. Her freckles were very dark against her pale skin. She tossed her head to throw her long hair back over her shoulders.

"You don't understand, do you?" He repeated the words *rip off*. "Means steal."

"How will my father get the keys?"

The boy sighed a how-can-anyone-be-so-stupid sigh. Clearly he was not only dealing with a foreigner, but one who was also not too bright.

"You're your father. Right?"

The girl nodded.

"You get off the train. You see the car. But—you find it locked. So what do you do? You ask yourself—'Self, if I were car keys where would I be?'"

"At the ticket window?"

"Abracadabra!"

Rynn smiled, then she remembered her broken tooth and stopped. "You *are* a magician!"

"Hell, I can make a whole chicken disappear!" The cape fairly snapped as he flourished it.

"I know where you got your name."

"Yeah?"

"Mario the Magician."

"Yeah?"

"Story," she said, "by Thomas Mann."

"Mario's my real name."

"Then it's double magic. Proves you love that story as much as I do."

"Never read it."

He went outside into the misty afternoon, using his cane like a golf stick, to putt a horse chestnut down the front path.

Rynn followed him, her hands thrust deep in the pockets of her duffle coat, to stand in the leaves.

"Look," he said. "I got to get going or I'll be late. As it is, I'll have to put my bike in the car and then go from the station."

She watched the absurd little moustache hanging loose. He was about to speak, but he stopped and pressed his upper lip to stick the dangling moustache in place. For the first time Rynn found herself looking at his hands. Small hands, slender, not much bigger than hers. She hated to see chewed fingernails, and the boy's were ragged down to the quick.

"You want to come that far with me?"

"Where?"

"The station."

"I have to stay here."

"Okay." The boy shrugged. He swung his golf club cane, lopping off mummified zinnia heads.

"How much do you charge to drive the car?"

"My father said to chalk it up to customer relations."

"That's very kind."

"No it isn't. Like I said, customer relations. He'll get it back on a new carburetor or some damn thing." He looked up into the branches. She sensed he had something else he wanted to say and the girl waited.

"You know you got a broken tooth?" Mario made no attempt to soften the announcement with a smile. He announced it as a fact, flatly, the way he had said that he was a cripple.

"How come I never see you in school?"

"I don't go to school."

"No?"

"No."

"Not at all?"

"I have never gone to school."

"You sick or something?"

"Why do you say that?"

"Like you're suffering from an incurable disease or something? I mean you've got to have an excuse."

"Because I don't go to school?" She brushed her hair back from her face. "School is stultifying."

"You haven't been so how would you know?" With his cane he poked through a gold leaf and lifted it up for a closer look. "*I'd* sort of miss it."

Rynn picked up her own leaf for study. "The only thing *I* miss is I'd adore to sit in on sex education. It might be amusing to hear how you Americans muck it up."

Rynn giggled, taking care to keep her tooth covered. Suddenly she wished very much she had said nothing about Americans or giggled, for Mario was turning away from her.

Her heart almost leaped when he turned back. "You know something? If you're *not* English, the way you talk and all, you're a real asshole."

The boy walked unevenly through the tree trunks toward the Bentley. Rynn watched him study the car. He turned and motioned for her to come to him.

Something held her from crossing the wet leaves to the car.

"Come here!" he called.

Fists in her duffle coat, she ran to the car. Mario was frowning, his moustache even more crooked than before.

"You said it was your father's car."

"What I *said* was he needed it at the station."

Mario's black eyes were boring straight into hers. Rynn met his gaze. The boy was the first to speak.

"It's hers."

"Meaning?" She watched her breath come out in steam as if to show Mario what he was saying was worth so little concentration.

"It's Mrs. Hallet's."

"Oh?" she said. It wasn't a very effective way to parry his statement, but she felt she had said it with convincing indifference.

"Her Bentley. Only thirty-four thousand miles. I ought to know, my father works on it."

"She's lending it to us."

"No she isn't." The boy was not smiling. He had the warm olive skin of so many Italians. Why did he have dark lines under his eyes?

The girl looked away under the pretext of peeling a wet red leaf from the car.

"No." He repeated the accusation.

"You simply cannot say *no* like that. You don't know—"

"You think you're putting me on, don't you? Only you're not."

Rynn's voice became very English, very aloof. "If you don't believe me, go into the house. Ring her. Ask *her*." She added an edge as if she were accustomed to giving orders. *"Right now!"*

She looked back to find Mario's black eyes staring into hers.

"She won't even let her own creep son drive it. *Or* my father—even after he tunes it."

"Well, she lets *my* father," Rynn said petulantly. Abruptly she changed her tone. "Look," she said, "you really are being awfully stupid."

"Tell me, does it hurt your throat to talk that way?"

The girl went scarlet.

"Talk about stupid. Wow. I mean what do you call it when you're the one who's asking *me* to do you the favor?"

The girl pulled her wallet from her coat pocket and drew out bills. "Here. Five whole dollars."

The boy turned from her and headed for the tree where his bicycle leaned.

"I'm already late for my magic show."

"Your father told you to drive this car!"

His hands on the bicycle's handlebars, Mario raised his black eyes slowly. "What's wrong with you?"

"Nothing's wrong!" Rynn would have given anything to have kept her voice from sounding so desperate.

"Like what time does your father's train get in?"

"Right away."

"You see?" The black eyes were still holding her. "There isn't a train till after six."

"Look. If I offended you about the money, I'm sorry. But it is true about the car."

"No it isn't."

He wheeled the bicycle from the tree. He adjusted a strap that held a large canvas bag marked MARIO THE MAGICIAN full of his show equipment on the back fender.

In the distance a crow complained in the mist.

Mario put his cane across the handlebars and climbed onto the bicycle. "I've got to do my show."

Rynn placed her boot in front of the tire to keep the bicycle from moving. "Come back after?"

Mario stared into her face.

"Please?"

She knew the boy was waiting for her to tell him the truth.

She reached out to straighten his moustache, but he twisted away.

"I'll fix it when I get there."

Rynn's eyes sought the boy's for as long as it took her to speak. "I need your help."

Mario looked down at his handlebars. He could have been a very little boy. "Maybe. I mean after I do my show."

"You promise?"

The bicycle rolled across the leaves and out into the lane.

9

THE FIRE crackled in the hearth. The gateleg table was set for dinner for two.

Rynn, tearing lettuce leaves and dropping them one by one into a salad bowl, looked across the counter to Mario's black cape which hung on the hall peg. The bicycle leaned against the wall. The boy himself had taken the telephone on its long cord and sat near the hearth talking to his mother. "The new trick really went over big. I'm still at the birthday party. They asked me to stay for dinner. Just hamburgers and cokes. Some of the kids in my class at school are here."

Rynn cut a tomato into wedges and dropped them into the bowl. She looked at the boy silhouetted by the fire. She had not asked him to lie about where he was, but she was glad he had.

"Tell Tom *he* can take her to the horrible movie for a change. It's his turn anyway. Bye." He hung up and brought the instrument to the kitchen counter and Rynn. "One thing about a big family, you've always got a little brother you can make drag your horrible sister to the horrible movie."

With a swiftness and expertise the boy pronounced sleight of hand, the girl sliced a cucumber.

"Don't you have any brothers or sisters?"

"No." She reached for the oil and vinegar.

"Wow. I mean that's something I can't even imagine."

"Will you light the candles, please?"

Until he returned to the coffee table she had forgotten the boy limped. He took matches from the cigarette box.

"You smoke?"

"Sometimes," she said tasting the salad dressing.

"You don't worry about cancer?"

She did not answer.

At the table Mario lit the candles, straightening them in their pewter candlesticks. The two flames wavered into life, the glasses and the silverware reflected their sparkle.

The barefoot girl carried a tray to the table. She had changed into her long white sheath with the blue border at the neck and sleeves, and as she moved from the dark kitchen into the fire's glow she knew she looked her best. She felt an added pride when she found Mario staring at her.

The match flame burned his finger and he quickly shook it out.

"You got all dressed up for dinner," he said.

"Changed from my Levis is all."

"Very pretty dress."

She looked down at the white sheath as if she had never noticed that it was, as he said, very pretty. "My father and I bought it in Morocco."

"They smoke a lot of hash there."

"They do a lot of things there." She managed to sound very worldly, an impression she enjoyed giving the boy.

"You ever smoke hash?"

The girl put the salad bowl on the table.

"Hundreds of times."

"Really?" Mario's admiration was undisguised.

She found something so touching, so innocent about his awe that she shook her head.

"Not really."

She hoped her honesty would put him at ease. He was being overly polite, showing with every move how eager he was to please, trying so hard to do the proper thing. Too many manners.

Rynn wondered, because his behavior was so forced—and remembering the way he asked his mother's permission to stay at the birthday party—if tonight might not be the first time Mario had ever eaten dinner with anyone but his enormous Italian family.

"You go ahead and sit down," she said running back to the kitchen.

But Mario stood, as she knew he would, until she brought the broiled lamb chops, buttered broccoli and parsley potatoes. He pulled back her chair, and after several awkward maneuvers they both hoped their laughter covered, he managed to settle the girl at the table.

Across from one another, they dropped napkins into their laps and smiled self-consciously. She pointed to his black tie.

"You're very formal."

"How about you?" He indicated her long dress.

With candle flames between them they both felt they were entering a new and rarefied world of men and women who dressed for dinner and dined by candlelight.

"We should have music," Rynn said.

She ran to the stereo, and when Julian Bream's guitar filled the parlor Mario looked in wonder at the source of overhead sound. Rynn was turning out all the lights till only the fire and the candles lit the room.

"You want wine?"

"Do you?"

"I hate it."

"Me too."

She saw that Mario was waiting for her to sit and begin eating, and she scrambled into her chair before he could help her. She made a little display of eating in order that the boy might begin with his broccoli and potatoes. They were easier to handle with a knife and fork than the two lamb chops. She knew he was watching her, fascinated by the way she held her knife and fork in what, to Americans, were the wrong hands. She was happy to show him the English had not the slightest difficulty getting the lamb off the bones.

They sat for a long moment without speaking—a silence filled by guitar music. At last Mario managed to get one bite of lamb on his fork.

"Very good," he said.

"Thank you."

She picked up a bone in her hands and nibbled. Mario again watched closely, then followed her example. She knew he was truly enjoying his meal now that he got fuller bites of meat.

"You're a really great cook."

"What's so surprising about that?"

"I only meant—for being thirteen and all."

Rynn tossed the lamb bone to her plate, and he realized he had said something to anger her. But what? She was glowering at him. He stopped gnawing his lamb bone.

"You're just as bad as the rest of them."

Mario was wise enough to say nothing.

"How old do you have to be before people treat you as a person? Cooking's not like a piece a clever child stands up and recites or a parlor trick one performs for the adults. Of course I can cook."

"I only meant that not even all grown-ups can cook."

"Anyone who can read can cook."

Rynn picked up her other chop.

Had the crisis passed?

"My Mom can't," Mario said. "She *buys* Italian spaghetti sauce. *Frozen*." He looked at the girl. Was she smiling?

He wished she would smile.

"Like we've got this big family joke." He looked across the candlelight. "You and your father have family jokes?"

"Of course."

"Well ours is that when my Mom's out in the kitchen getting dinner, we always say 'dinner's thawing.' Then we always say, 'But Mom isn't.' "

Rynn did not laugh.

"Because of all the frozen food she uses."

"I understand."

The boy put his meat on his plate and wiped his greasy fingers on his napkin.

"Supposed to be hysterically funny." He looked at her. "The English got some kind of law against laughing?"

"That was very funny," she said without conviction.

Now it was Mario who threw his napkin on the table.

"Shit."

Julian Bream's guitar evoked a summer night in Spain. For a long moment Rynn sat and Mario pushed his fork at his broccoli. Then she spoke, her voice as quiet as a whisper, "Mario the Magician?"

"Yeah?"

"Thank you. About the car I mean."

"That's okay."

"Then eat your chop."

"It's very good."

But he did not eat.

"You don't like to smile, do you?" Evidently he felt it was

his turn to be cruel. "I mean that way you have to show your chipped tooth."

"Let me worry about that."

"You think I care? My oldest brother got *all* of his upper front teeth knocked out playing football. He smiles. He smiles his goddamn head off."

"Eat your chop."

"Okay."

Mario picked up the meat.

"I wasn't really all that certain you would come back." Rynn scraped up a drop of warm candle wax.

"Your big hang-up," Mario said from around his lamb, "is that you don't trust guys."

"Why did you?"

"Come back?"

"No. The other."

"The car?"

"You didn't have to."

"Damn right I didn't."

Mario leaned back in his chair. He could see his father settling back at the dinner table, demanding silence, working up to the Big Man statement. His father had the advantage of a cigar.

"If you really want to know, it's mostly because you may be very smart, but you're stupid. Look—if you really wanted to get her car away from the front of your house why go to all the hassle of taking it to the station? See, the trick in magic is to do the one thing that's so simple and so obvious no one ever thinks of it."

"What's so simple and obvious?"

"What's simpler than putting it back where it came from? I mean you did say her office is where she drove it from."

Rynn knew she had not thought out this part of the plan very well. No, it was not a plan. It was an emergency, and he had helped her. He had done what she asked him to do. He had done what he felt he *could* do. Still, she hated not having a plan, not being in command, not knowing every single step of what had been done.

"Anybody see you leave it at her office?"

"Jesus," he said, abandoning his lamb bone. "You think I want to get busted for ripping off Old Lady Hallet's most prized possession? Like if I'd been dumb enough to get caught she'd have my ass in jail for eight hundred and twenty-seven years." He pushed his knife and fork across his plate with a clatter. "I mean if you don't trust me, why the hell didn't *you* do it?" He folded his arms. "But you don't even trust me enough to tell me *why* I did it."

"You did it to help me."

"Yeah." The boy shrugged. Somehow the simple truth no longer seemed enough now to cover the enormous chance he had taken. There was also another truth of which he did not speak, that he did not know any other girl who had ever asked him to do anything.

"You should have put the keys through the mailbox in the office door."

"No I shouldn't."

Rynn poked at her lamb, then laid her knife and fork across the plate.

"Here I am," Mario said, "sitting there in her Bentley in front of her horrible goddamn office. In the horrible goddamn dark. Trying like mad not to have anybody see me. Trying not to get busted. 'Keep it simple,' I said to myself. Yeah, that sounds easy, then all of a sudden it hits me. Okay, so I may not know why Mrs. Hallet didn't drive her own car back, but one thing I do know. Mrs. Hallet wouldn't put her own car keys through no horrible goddamn door mailbox. Not for her creep son to get. She'd keep her keys. They'd be wherever she is."

"When you left, you locked the car door?"

"All four." Reaching into his pocket, he pulled out the keys and jingled them in front of the girl. "They'd be wherever she is. Since you won't tell me *that*—here, you take the horrible goddamn keys."

They fell with a clink where he dropped them on her plate.

"Give them to her the next time you see her."

Rynn picked up the keys, jingled them as if to feel their presence, and closed her fist around them. All at once, as if she had had all the talk of the car she could stand, she pushed back her chair and rose to her feet.

"I feel like wine."

"Me too," said Mario as she ran into the kitchen.

"Red or white?"

"Anything but dago red."

A cupboard door banged. Rynn hurried back to the table holding a bottle.

"*Voila!* You be the father and open it."

"Very fancy. Like this one doesn't unscrew. Got a cork and everything."

She handed him the opener.

Digging into the cork, Mario stopped smiling. Now, not having to look at her, he was again about to ask the question she did not want him to ask.

"Rynn . . ."

"One rule with the wine. We can't discuss anything serious."

He was not going to be stopped that easily.

"You haven't told me why . . ."

Rynn stepped back from the table and her bare feet turned in half a dozen steps of a dance as she lifted her hair and piled it on top of her head.

"My *darling*," her voice was a fluting parody of a very-upper-class-English-woman she had laughed at in a play on television in London. "That just so *happens* to be an *extraordinary* vintage, so *do—do* show the *greatest*, the *utmost* care."

"How come she didn't drive it back?"

Rynn insisted on maintaining her fantasy as one hand wafted in the direction of the bottle. "A nineteen-oh-*two*."

"*Rynn?*"

At once, she let her hair fall, and her voice took on a surprisingly sharp little bite.

"I told you. You did it because I asked you to."

"You made it sound like a matter of life and death. You said we didn't have time to talk about it—*then!*"

"*You didn't have to!*" Her voice was shrill.

"I risked my goddamn ass for you!"

She glared at him coldly. "All you did was drive her car back—"

"*Why didn't she?*" Mario had never sounded more demanding. "Look. You better tell me what the hell's going on. Because if I had left that car of hers at the station like you told me to, everybody in the village would have recognized it."

"They'd think she'd taken the train into New York!"

"No they wouldn't. Everybody knows Mrs. Hallet hates New York. Too many foreigners. Mrs. Hallet wouldn't set foot in New York." He caught the girl staring at him. "You didn't know that, did you?"

Rynn grabbed the bottle from his hand, splashing wine on her white caftan. She poured a glass and gulped its contents.

"I hate it," she said banging the glass down.

"You don't trust anybody, do you?"

"My father."

The boy shrugged, and took a sip of wine. "Yeah, well,

lots of luck." A glance at the girl told him she had not de-
tected his sarcasm. She had left the conversation and was
miles away. He picked up the wine bottle.

"More?"

She shook her head.

"Don't like it?"

"Sour."

In defiance he drank more wine.

"Another lamb chop?"

When he answered he watched the effect of his words.
"How about saving some for your father?"

"I told you. He's not coming home till later."

"Shouldn't we still save him some?"

"He's staying in New York."

"You never said that."

Mario's eyes never left her. She rose from her chair and
brought a plate with more meat from the kitchen. With a
serving fork she dropped a lamb chop on his plate.

"I'm glad you're here," she said. She stood beside his chair.
Mario did not turn to speak; he looked straight at the
gnawed bone.

"You ever stayed alone before?"

"Hundreds of times."

"Like all those times you smoked hash?"

The stereo clicked off. In the corner Gordon's sharp little
claws scrabbled on the wire of his cage.

"You're not scared?"

"Of what?"

"Being alone."

"Haven't you ever been alone?"

"With eleven brothers and sisters?"

She sat.

"You must have a big house."

"What we have," he said, "is that bunch of rooms that

used to be a motel in back of the garage. The only time we're all together is when we sit down for one of my Mom's rotten dinners. You should see all of us. Wow. Nice and squalid."

"Twelve kids plus Mom and Dad feeding their faces? I should hate it."

He picked up the lamb chop and gnawed it to the bone. "Better than being alone."

Rynn moved from Mario's chair to the fireplace.

"Never less idle than when completely idle, never less alone than when completely alone." She did not seem to be talking to him so much as reassuring herself.

Mario, examining the bone, shrugged, showing he was not impressed.

"Cicero said that," she announced.

"Yeah? Well I didn't ask what Cicero said. I asked about you."

"Cicero and I, we agree."

"About being alone."

"Quite."

Mario half turned in his chair. The girl was gazing at him. "I'm not sure that's normal."

"Maybe not for you."

"Say you're here all alone and something happened?"

"Like what?"

"Things. Things can happen. Like there was this old woman over in Sag Harbor who they found strangled to death with a body stocking."

Mario looked at the girl to see if she was smiling. There was no smile on the white face that stared into the fire. He went to the front window and peered between the curtains into the dark.

"You know you got an outside light?"

"I never looked."

In the hall Mario found a panel of switches. He flicked them until they saw a spotlight shine behind the curtains.

"From now on, leave it on at night. Okay?"

"Okay."

He came back into the sitting room.

"And thank you."

"For what?"

"For worrying."

"Like I said, that's okay." He went to the other window and looked out. "You got a gun?"

"No."

"You should have."

"My father says having a gun is far more dangerous than not having a gun."

"*My* father has a gun."

Rynn crossed to the corner where Gordon rattled his cage.

"You Americans are a violent people."

"What do you want me to do about it?"

"Finish your dinner."

Mario went to the table but instead of returning to his dinner, he picked up his napkin and draped it over his fist. He reached into the fireplace to dip an index finger into the soot and dab two eyes and a mouth on his knuckles, to create a fist puppet which he brought close to Rynn's face. The mouth opened and an old woman spoke with a French accent.

"Mademoiselle, that was a marvelous dinner. *Merci.*"

Rynn bent close to speak to the old-woman puppet.

"Only that wasn't French," she said to the face. "That was English cooking."

The old woman's voice changed. The face waggled, the crumpled mouth opened, and a voice so English came out that Rynn applauded.

"Was it now! Then I *should* say—how *absolutely* smashing!"

Rynn giggled.

Mario had yet to get her to open her mouth in a full laugh.

"You're very good!" she said applauding.

"Part of the act. Mr. Show Biz—that's me."

She ran to the cage and lifted out the rat. "You should have more of an audience. Meet Gordon."

"How do you do, Gordon," the fist, an English woman, said.

Rynn kissed the rat. "Isn't Gordon super?"

"Super!" the fist waggled at the rat.

"I love Gordon."

Mario tore the napkin off and tossed it onto the table. He brushed the soot from the back of his hand and reached for the pet. "Let me?"

Rynn held the rat, hesitating.

"You can at least trust me with your rat."

She handed Gordon to Mario. "You have any pets?"

"Just my parents."

She giggled again. "Lovely."

"Which I feed and water regularly."

"Teaches you responsibility."

They both giggled. Rynn kissed Gordon's pink nose. The boy carried the rat to the table. The white whiskers quivered as Gordon found a shred of lamb. As they stood side by side at the table watching Gordon nibble, they were aware of their closeness. Neither moved.

"If I tell you why I'm crippled, will you tell about the car?"

The girl did not look away from Gordon.

"No," she said.

"I have so many brothers and sisters my mother forgot who did and who didn't have polio shots."

"Is that supposed to be funny?"

"Now you have to tell me about the car."

Rynn moved away from the boy. She was creating another fantasy woman. Not a great lady this time but a cockney.

"*I* never 'ad me no brother or a sister. We was so poor my dad 'ad to use newspapers, old manuscripts even, for nappies—*diapers* to you."

"Anything to keep from telling the truth. Is that it?"

She looked into the kitchen as if to forestall any other questions.

"Would you care for a sweet? There's some lovely ice cream. Peach."

"I'm stuffed."

"So is Gordon. Look at him." The pink claws scuttled across the table top to the edge, pink eyes raised to look at the girl. She reached out and picked up her pet. "In the car . . ." she began in an offhand voice.

"*Her* car?" Mario was determined not to allow the girl to be offhand. "Some car. All that deep leather upholstery. I mean you don't find plastic madonnas on the dashboards of cars like that."

"In her car"—she was returning Gordon to his cage, and this time she did not wait for Mario to interrupt—"did you leave fingerprints?"

When Mario hobbled to his cape in the hall, again the girl was shocked. Again she had forgotten he used a cane. She saw him pull gloves out of a pocket and draw them on. Waving both gloved hands he limped back to her.

"Presto! No fingerprints!"

"Mario the Magician!"

He spread his hands, an entertainer coming out on the stage and introducing himself to his audience. "In person!"

He performed his bullfighter's pass and flung the cape over his shoulders.

Rynn clapped her applause.

"Do a trick!"

"Ladies and Gentlemen, I shall now make an automobile disappear!"

The girl patted an extravagantly theatrical yawn and sighed her boredom. "But you already did that."

"Then behold. *I* shall disappear!"

"You think you can?"

"The Greatest Magician in the World? Close your eyes and count to three."

"Okay," she said.

The boy did not move.

"Close them tight. Ready?"

Rynn nodded.

"One," Mario said as he looked around and saw the couch. "Two," he called as he hurried around the couch and sank out of sight.

"Three." His voice, sepulchral and disembodied, hung in the room. "You may now open your eyes."

Rynn opened her eyes and gazed about. She laughed and clapped in more applause. Then she stopped laughing.

"Mario?" a hint of apprehension was in her voice. She did not move.

"Can you reappear?"

The room was silent for only an instant before her next call, sharp with fear.

"*Mario?*"

She looked around the room. She ran to the foot of the stairs to the second floor.

"Mario?"

She had reached the studio door and was about to turn the knob when Mario, popping up from behind the couch, snapped open Mrs. Hallet's candy-stripe umbrella and thrust it high.

"Mary Fucking Poppins!"

For Rynn every bit of the fun of the game's make-believe fear, the excitement of only a moment ago, was gone. She rushed at the boy. Her voice was a shriek.

"Give me that!"

But Mario, still in the excitement, failed to realize she had ended the game. He laughed at Rynn's shout. When she cried out for the umbrella he felt she was adding a new wildness to the excitement. Teasing her with the umbrella, he poked it at her, jabbed it, snapped it open and shut. He taunted. He jeered.

"Come and get it!"

The girl dashed onto the couch and clutched with both hands at the umbrella, but Mario waved it, shook it, jerked it out of her reach. Clambering the length of the couch she grasped at his every move.

"Stop it!" her voice was hard, her arms lunging.

The striped folds, like some wild creature fighting back, snapped open and shut at her.

She climbed down from the couch and drove the boy to the hearth and into the corner where Gordon scratched in his cage. Rynn, now in tears, arms flailing, grasping at any movement, a child in a game of keepaway frustrated almost to the point of hysteria, grasped and clawed.

With an explosion of laughter Mario broke from the corner pushing past Rynn in a dash to get past the coffee table. His cane clattered. He stumbled and sprawled on the floor. Rynn threw herself on him, tearing at the umbrella. Struggling, rocking together, they rose. The boy worked his arms around her in a hammerlock pinning her against him, helpless. His cape fell over both of them as Rynn twisted frantically, grasping for the umbrella.

The fire glowed and the candles burned, their combined light holding the shadows in the corners. Outside the front window the spotlight shone through the curtains.

Rynn struggled against him. Nothing moved but the wavering glow from the flames.

Rynn was the first to see it. Mario felt her stiffen in his arms, and go cold.

Against the curtains a shadow raced.

"Sshh," she whispered. "Listen."

"Somebody's there!"

As Mario released her she grabbed the umbrella and without a sound lifted the cover of the woodbox and dropped it inside. Noiselessly she lowered the cover. The two shrank from the window.

Mario was straining to hear whatever was there, what had filled first the girl and now him with trembling.

She whispered again. "Put out the candles!"

He reached the table and pinched out the flames. Now only the fire cast its dim red light into the room to be swallowed in dark around them. He sank to the floor beside the girl, and they huddled together in front of the fire.

Both watched the window.

Then they saw what they dreaded most to see.

10

THEY CROUCHED, huddled together so many minutes—hours?—breathing as one, their eyes never leaving the curtains—that as each minute passed, as their hearts slowed pounding in their throats, they were more and more tempted to believe they had only imagined seeing the shadow.

Rynn was the first to rise. Mario pushed himself to his feet and the only sound either of them made as they moved to the window was the tap of the cane. The boy reached out to part the curtains.

"Careful." Rynn's voice was low.

Both faces pressed against the cold glass.

"Can you see anything?" she asked.

Mario's breath made a damp spot which he wiped away with his cape.

"Out there—in the lane."

"What?" She strained to peer beyond the screen of bare branches.

The boy pulled Rynn from the curtains which fell back into place. He spoke without whispering.

"Police car."

Rynn sank against him sighing with relief. But almost at once, as if she dared not believe his statement, she turned again to peer out.

Mario limped to the hall where he switched on the light.

Rynn raced to his side. At the door she stifled a cry and shrank against him, for just as she reached for the latch, a knock thudded on the other side of the door.

"You want to open it or shall I?" he asked.

"You open it."

"It'll look better if you do. I mean it's your house."

"Are you sure it's the police?"

Mario nodded.

Rynn expected to see a man in uniform. When she found a tall man in a black-and-white checked jacket and gray trousers standing before her she did not recognize him.

"Hey!" Mario cried from behind the girl. "You know who this is? My Uncle Ron!"

Officer Miglioriti smiled at Rynn and now she saw it was indeed the officer. He was smiling the same smile which on Mario was almost too pretty.

"Hi," the girl said, her hand reaching out for the man's. Without turning to Mario, she explained, "We've already met." Stepping back from the door she was suddenly the hostess.

"Please, won't you come in?"

Miglioriti's glance included Mario who still wore his black cape. The boy, deep in admiration of her grown-up assurance, was watching Rynn.

"We were just now having some wine," she said, the most accomplished of English hostesses. "Will you join us?"

Miglioriti ran his fingers through his thick black hair.

"No thanks."

Mario, stripping off his cape, spoke to his uncle. "You're off duty, right?"

The officer surveyed the room where the table had been set for two. He looked at the boy.

"What happened?" Mario demanded in a kind of banter that Rynn had often heard young people use with older people in the States, a familiarity she rarely heard in England. "I mean it's Saturday night," the boy's tone was close to mocking. "Your Playmate of the Week split?"

Miglioriti, not at all annoyed, stated flatly, "She's waiting out in the car."

Mario, at Rynn's side, moved his hands describing curves. "He likes the ones who look like they were blown up with a bicycle pump."

"Ask her in," said Rynn.

"Can't stay," Miglioriti glanced again at the boy. Was he annoyed that he was unable to speak to the girl alone?

"Perhaps just a splash of wine?"

"Half a glass."

"Think Miss Thirty-six, twenty-eight, thirty-six will wait?" Mario grinned.

Rynn shut the door and the three moved to the table where Rynn poured the officer a full glass of wine, and the man thanked her.

There was a silence for a full ten seconds, as Miglioriti stared at the dinner plates, the lamb bones, cold broccoli.

"She asked me to dinner," Mario explained. "Really terrific. She cooked it all herself."

Miglioriti picked up the bottle of wine. He looked at it, an investigator weighing a clue in a detective story.

"Enjoy the wine, did you?" the officer asked the boy.

"What are you going to do? Bust us for drinking under age?"

Miglioriti was directing his remarks only at Mario.

"You're just lucky I don't smell any grass."

"Got any?" Mario grinned and shot a conspiratorial look at Rynn.

Now Miglioriti included the girl. "Like I was saying, right? No respect for the law."

The boy tossed his cape on the couch. "Look who wants respect. When all the time *he's* using a police car for personal business." Mario knew he had scored off his uncle, and he allowed himself his widest grin.

"Holler police corruption," Miglioriti said drinking and putting the glass on the table where he studied the two place settings.

"Just the two of you?"

"Her father's asleep," Mario said, a little too quickly, as Rynn's eyes shot to his for a split second.

Again Miglioriti's voice only barely concealed the tones of a detective cross-examining a suspect. "You meet Rynn's father?"

As if to emphasize that the boy was on his own, that he would have to answer his uncle's question, Rynn left the table to sit on the couch.

Mario picked up the bottle and poured himself a full glass. "Sure."

Rynn felt her heart tighten.

"He have dinner with you?"

"Does it look like it?" Mario pulled a chair back from the table and sat. "What's this supposed to be? Some kind of third degree?" The boy drank his wine.

Rynn knew the officer was waiting for a more direct answer.

"No dinner?"

"He was so tired he went right to bed."

"I thought you said he was in his study working."

"I didn't say that. I said he was asleep."

Miglioriti turned to Rynn. "That's right. Rynn's the one who told me he was working."

She said, "That was this afternoon. After he finished his translating, he took it into town."

"Round trip in one day," Mario said. "Very tiring."

Miglioriti was at the stereo set. He read the name of the record. He turned and looked at the room.

"Dinner for two. Candlelight. Wine. Very romantic."

Over the rim of his wine glass, Mario looked at his uncle, but he spoke to Rynn.

"Just because he's practically a sex maniac he thinks a guy can't even finish dinner with a girl before he has to make out."

Miglioriti smiled his marvelous smile at Rynn. "If he doesn't try, tell me and I'll have the family disown him."

Rynn responded with the giggle she felt was expected.

Mario shook his head and sighed as if to show how little his uncle understood life.

"Talk." He intended his world-weary reflection for the girl's benefit, but his uncle could listen if he was not too old to learn. "Italians *talk* a lot about sex—"

Miglioriti held up a hand. He was finished with the banter.

Rynn could see the man was deadly serious. Waiting for him to speak, she readied herself for more questions about her father. The officer would want to know why she was alone. She was ready. But she was not ready for what Miglioriti said.

"Frank Hallet called."

The huge man moved to the fire to warm his hands.

"Around six. He was worried about his mother. Said she hadn't come home. He called again around eight."

"Old Lady Hallet," Mario said, "is probably out house-pimping."

Miglioriti looked at Rynn. "Mario here doesn't like the Hallets."

"Does anybody?"

"Other Hallets," the man said.

"Wrong," said Mario. "Tell her why he had to get married."

"Don't be a smartass."

Mario carried his glass of wine to the couch.

"Ask him," the boy said to Rynn, "about the time he tried to get him busted for dragging some little girl into the bushes. After that his mother married him off to some cocktail waitress with two kids."

"That's enough."

"To prove he was normal."

"You are a smartass."

"How about what he tried to pull with that girl in Junior High, the one with these really big tits—"

"You tell that story again and I will personally knock the snot out of you."

Mario chuckled into his wine.

"Normal. Wow! About as normal as a three-dollar bill!"

Miglioriti had had all he wanted of Mario; he made that clear by speaking only to Rynn.

"When Hallet called at six to report he couldn't find his mother I figured she was out, like smartass here said, with a real-estate prospect, showing a house. When he called back at eight it began to look like something was wrong."

"How do you know she still isn't out?" Mario would not be excluded.

"Her Bentley's in front of her office."

"Maybe they took the prospect's car."

Rynn wished she could turn and show Mario the confidence his answer inspired.

But the officer demolished that confidence.

"If you knew Mrs. Hallet, you'd know she never rides in a stranger's car. She only takes her own. Ask me why, I might even tell you."

"Thinks somebody's going to rape her?" Mario chuckled.

"She takes her own car because on her side of the front seat she carries a forty-five Magnum."

Mario shrugged to show his cool. "She got a license? Bet she hasn't. *Bust* her!"

"*Zitti!*"

"Italian for *shut up*." The boy tapped Rynn's shoulder. "Police brutality, see?" To his uncle he said, "I got a witness."

Again Miglioriti tried to ignore his nephew and talk only to Rynn. "Hallet reported you called. Something about his mother coming over here to pick up some glasses for jelly-making."

Both Miglioriti and Mario waited for her answer.

The girl glanced at the carton against the wall. "They're still waiting for her."

Miglioriti drew the carton from the wall and opened the lid. The glasses clinked as his foot pushed the carton back.

"She never came by?"

"After I called," the girl said, "I didn't leave the house." She thought back. The truth was, she had left the house only to take the walk. No one had seen her but the kids coming back from the football game, and their car had not been close enough that they would remember seeing what she looked like. Her lie would hold.

"I was here all the time."

"I called Hallet back about half an hour ago," Miglioriti said. "His wife said she still wasn't home."

"So you came looking for her here?" asked Mario.

For a long moment neither of them thought the officer was going to answer the question.

"No. I came here because I thought Rynn might be alone."

It was Mario who asked what they both were thinking.

"And you figured that creep might decide to come out here?"

Miglioriti's big blunt fingers plowed through his hair.

"So I took the patrol car. Okay with you, smartass?"

Mario spread his hands as a magician would to show that nothing was concealed. "Only she's not alone."

"I may be a cop, but I can still see."

"Thank you," Rynn said.

Miglioriti poured another splash of wine.

"Everything okay?"

"Fine," the girl said.

"Uncle Ron?"

The officer drank the wine and put the glass on the table.

"I know. You don't want me to tell your mom and dad you were here."

"Like if you didn't"—the boy grinned—"I mean would that automatically mean the collapse of Western Civilization?"

"If you want my help, don't be a smartass."

Mario's spread fingers flattened against his chest—the innocent unjustly accused.

"Who's a smartass?"

The officer spoke to Rynn. "I don't know. Maybe *you* can teach him some manners."

Suddenly Mario sounded like a little boy. "You won't tell Mom and Dad? They think I'm at this birthday party—"

"Because that's what you told them? You've already incriminated yourself." Miglioriti was smiling again, but the smile was for Rynn alone.

"In a good cause." His smile faded. "About Mrs. Hallet. I'd appreciate any help you can give."

"I know," Rynn said, every bit as serious as he. "I only wish I *could* help. . . ."

If Miglioriti wasn't satisfied with the answers, he had nothing further to say. "Thanks for the wine."

The man moved quickly through the parlor and out the door.

Rynn ran after him and called from the porch.

"Good-night!" In the cold, her voice turned to mist, and Mario pulled her inside. He shut the door, holding a silencing finger to his lips. They would wait in silence long enough for the policeman to reach his car and drive away.

Only when he heard the engine start did Mario let his pent-up fear explode.

"Wowie! What was it like for you? Scary, uh? I mean wasn't it . . ."

But Rynn had turned away from him and seemed to be calmly pouring a glass of wine. She held it out to Mario who grabbed it and gulped.

"I mean how's a guy going to know who it might be out there. Right?"

The girl picked drops of wax from the table beneath the candlesticks.

"There was no reason to be frightened."

Mario blinked and shook his head to show he could scarcely believe she could sound so calm.

"You can say that now. But you were scared. Man, you were scared *shitless!*"

Why was she refusing to share the thrill of this moment? Mario threw his cape over his shoulders. He clapped his silk hat on his head. He waved his abracadabra cane.

"How did you like the way I made your father disappear?"

"You lied."

"Bet your ass. What did you want me to do?"

He could not think why she would refuse to share his excitement, why she would withhold credit for the way he had held up under his uncle's cross-examination.

Angrily he adjusted his cape, set his hat at a rakish angle, and smacked the floor with his cane. He was marching the few steps toward the door when Rynn said, "Where do you think you're going?" If she was fighting panic her voice betrayed none of it.

He neither turned nor answered. He knew she was watching his every step and he used his cane to make his way, as straight as he was able, directly for the door.

Rynn rushed after him.

He turned. His grin was huge.

"Just testing. Like you don't really want me to go or anything, do you?"

She shook her head no.

"Righto," he said in his cheeriest English voice. As his arm slipped around her, Rynn threw her head back and burst into giggles that she let grow into roars of laughter. She knew he was looking at her chipped tooth, but she went right on laughing. Mario began to laugh too. Soon both were laughing till they fell into each other's arms and clung together.

Mario was the first to stop.

"Listen!"

Rynn, too, heard the knock at the door.

"Jesus," the boy said in a whisper. "He's back!"

Rynn stopped at the door with one hand on the latch. She waved to Mario to watch her handle the officer.

She threw the door wide.

Frank Hallet stood on the porch.

11

She fought to cover her rush of fear. She fought, too, to make some sense of what had happened. The policeman had come to this same door, but he had driven off down the lane. The shadow that flickered across the curtain had not been the officer's. All the time Miglioriti had been drinking wine with Rynn and Mario, Hallet had been at the house. Hallet had been waiting.

The man in the doorway smoothed long strands of tangled hair over his gleaming bald head. His watery blue eyes betrayed his share of surprise at the sight of the bicycle in the hall. His eyes shot to the sitting room to find the boy in the cape.

Hallet made no move. Behind him, out in the black night, the bare branches moved in the wind, scraping and clacking together.

Rynn prayed the man could not see how her legs shook under her caftan. Usually so quick to take action, so calm, so inventive with answers, she had no move to make, nothing to say. When she heard the *tap-tap* of Mario's cane, when she remembered that unlike every other night, she was not alone tonight, she blessed Mario in silence.

Mario tapped his way to stand at her side.

Hallet made the first move. Neither Rynn nor Mario knew how to stop him.

Now it was too late to shut him out.

He made no sign, no gesture, he uttered no command, but at each step he took into the hall, Rynn and Mario stumbled back. He was here. He needed to do nothing more to show them he was master of this place. At the strong scent of cologne Rynn stifled a wave of nausea.

Hallet's hands, usually pink, now glowed an angry red from the cold, and he kneaded them together as he approached the bicycle. He stared at the machine as if such a thing had never been seen in a house.

Rynn and Mario found themselves retreating into the parlor, moving when the man moved, stumbling back when he advanced.

Not until Hallet stood on the braided rug did he stop. Here he drew the tiny tube of ointment from his pocket and slid its shine over his heavy lips. In the same way he had stared at the bicycle, he now glanced around the room, focusing first on the couch, then the rocking chair, the woodbox, the table, as if this were the first time he had looked at these things. Almost unconsciously he smoothed a wrinkle from the braided rug with his suede shoes. One step took him to the wall and the cardboard carton. The suede shoe prodded the box. Glasses clinked.

"Jelly glasses?" he asked without turning to look at the girl.

She nodded yes.

At the table he picked up one of the pewter candlesticks and a pink finger probed the still warm wax. He turned the pewter in his hand before he set it down beside the two dinner plates, the wine glasses, the stained and crumpled napkins.

"Only two for dinner?"

He unbuttoned his raincoat, stripped it off, and flung it to the surprised boy. The man's jacket was of the same rough tweed as his mother's coat. The high collar of a frayed red turtleneck sweater pressed against his plump chin. His gray flannel trousers were even more rumpled than they had been the evening of Halloween, his suede shoes even muddier.

Neither youngster answered his question. Apparently he did not expect an answer, for he reached down to the coffee table and the cigarette box. Slowly he lifted out a Gauloise and held it upright in his finger tips. Deliberately, he moved his pink hand with the cigarette closer to Rynn till she recoiled to keep hand and cigarette from touching her face.

What did he want of her? What did he expect her to do? Hallet was sniffing the air. He turned his head, but he did not detect what he sought.

"Your father hasn't been smoking?"

Was it another question like the first, or did he now expect an answer?

Hallet sat in the rocking chair. He snapped his fingers at the boy.

Mario, still carrying the raincoat, limped to the coffee table, found the box of matches, and offered them to the man.

He shook his head, *no.*

The boy struck a flame and brought it to the chair and lit the man's cigarette.

Hallet drew deeply of the smoke and let it curl slowly up his face, silent as an idol in front of which incense burned. He rocked slowly.

Just as Rynn began to wonder if the man would ever speak, he rose from the rocker.

"It's cold," he said moving to the woodbox to get a log for the fire. His hand was on the lid.

Mario stifled a gasp. His eyes darted toward Rynn. He could see the girl staring at the box, rigid with fear, dreading the moment the man would raise the lid, the moment he would find the candy-stripe umbrella.

Rynn pushed past Hallet to reach the hearth.

"Let me put a log on the fire," she said in a voice that betrayed nothing of what Mario knew she felt.

Hallet shrugged and hearing Gordon's claws scraping on the wire mesh, moved to the corner.

Mario crowded onto the hearth to block Hallet's view of the box. With the girl, he lifted out two maple logs, quickly closed the box, pushed the wood into the fire and poked the embers under the logs into life. Quickly, Rynn maneuvered past him to sit on the woodbox. The smell of smoke was sharp.

The man lifted the squeaking white rat from his cage. "Gordon?"

The girl nodded.

"You love Gordon?"

She nodded again.

"I asked you a question."

"Yes."

"Yes what?"

"Yes, I love Gordon." Her voice was as cold and bitter as the night outside the door.

Only Gordon's head poked out from the red fist that held him tight. Hallet raised the tiny animal to the level of his blue eyes till the pink and white nose quivered in the curling cigarette smoke, the little red eyes rolled about wildly searching for a way to escape.

"I think Gordon loves you," Hallet said.

With his free hand the man flicked the ash from his cigarette and held it to his shiny lips, drawing in smoke until the end glowed red with fire. With a firm grip on the cigarette, he brought the burning end toward the white rat.

Rynn strangled a cry.

Hallet pressed the glowing cigarette against one of Gordon's eyes.

The rat screeched.

Rynn's hands smothered her scream.

"Jesus," Mario whispered.

As the rat screeched again and again and again the girl grabbed at Mario and buried her face in his cape. The boy's arm, though shaking, went around her shoulders.

Hallet held the cigarette up and blew on the end till the fire glowed. Only when the tobacco was a bright ember did he press it against the screeching rat's other eye. For a second he studied Gordon writhing in his hand, then tossed the creature into the fire.

He flicked the cigarette into the hearth.

Hallet thrust a hand in front of the girl's face. Torn marks in the plump palm oozed blood.

"Son of a bitch scratched me."

He told the boy to get him a disinfectant.

"In the medicine cabinet upstairs?" Mario asked. Trembling, Rynn could make no answer.

Mario limped across the room, hung the raincoat in the hall, and climbed the stairs.

Inspecting the scratches on his hand, Hallet stood before the girl with the air of a man who has satisfied himself with a good job of work. He lowered himself into the rocker and slowly brought the chair full tilt toward Rynn until he breathed in her face.

"Now. Where's your father?"

The girl muttered a single word.

"I can't hear you!"

"Sleeping," the girl managed to say.

"Upstairs?"

She shook her head.

"I asked you if he was upstairs."

"Next room." Her voice was barely audible.

Hallet pushed the sleeve of his tweed jacket from his wrist and glanced at his wristwatch.

"He goes to bed early."

"He was up all night. Translating."

"Yes?" The man was able to give the word a twist that meant, while her statement might be true, he did not for a minute believe it.

"Where? That room?" He jerked his head in the direction of the study.

"Yes."

"How many did you have for dinner?"

Rynn could still not bring herself to look at the man.

"You can see."

"I asked."

"Two."

"Only the two of you?"

Rynn nodded. Before the man spoke sharply, and she knew he would, she added, "Yes."

"Father?"

"No."

"No what?"

"My father didn't eat. . . ." She fought back tears.

"You said he was tired."

"Yes."

Mario had come downstairs and noiselessly entered the room. Holding the bottle of disinfectant, he limped toward the man.

Hallet turned to the boy. "Good dinner?"

Mario, too, spoke in a voice scarcely more than an audible whisper. "Yes."

Hallet grabbed the disinfectant.

"All alone?"

The boy shot a frantic glance at Rynn as if, in her face, he could read what she had said. But she had turned to face the corner.

"No."

"Alone, but not alone?" The man painted the scratches on his palm with red disinfectant from the tiny bottle.

"If you're not alone, where is he?"

"Who?"

"Who we're talking about." Hallet held his hand close to the light. "Her father."

"He's in the next room," Rynn, who could smell the disinfectant, said suddenly.

"Not upstairs?"

"No."

"You said upstairs."

"No I didn't."

"Not upstairs." Hallet finished painting his hand. He screwed the top back and held the bottle out to the waiting boy.

"Where he works?"

"Yes."

"Not working this time. Sleeping."

The girl nodded. Quickly she said, "Yes."

"But *not* upstairs," the man stated this as one who wants to make it perfectly clear he does not wish to make any mistakes.

Hallet rose from the rocker that creaked slowly back and forth. At the hearth he picked up the poker and stirred the fire. He spoke to the girl sitting on the woodbox, but a jerk of his head indicated the boy.

"He's?"

"I'm Mario Podesta."

Hallet did not look at the boy. He was facing Rynn. "I asked *you*."

"He's Mario Podesta."

Slowly he turned to the boy.

"That right?"

The boy nodded, but quickly added, "Yes."

"I've seen you around."

"My uncle," the boy said. "He's a cop."

"Yes."

"He was just here."

Hallet snapped his fingers for Mario to raise his eyes and look at him. "Why?"

"He's coming back."

"That isn't what I asked you."

"Tell him," said Rynn.

"Yes, tell me," Hallet said.

"He came here because he said you called him. Asking about your mother. Why she wasn't home. He thought you might come here looking for her."

"Why would she be here?" A hand, striped with red, signaled Rynn not to answer. He wanted to hear it from the boy.

"Those jelly glasses over there. She was coming by to pick them up."

"And there they are," said Hallet.

"Officer Miglioriti's coming back," Rynn said.

"Is that what he said?"

"Yes."

"I'm sure," Hallet said carefully settling himself into the rocker, "one day he will."

12

H<small>ALLET GLANCED</small> at his watch. "Where do you suppose that mother of mine could be keeping herself this time of night?" As he rocked, it could have been a trick of the wavering firelight, but Rynn was certain the man was smiling.

He held his pink hands out to the fire.

"The other night," he said, his face bright red in the firelight, "you said you didn't have any boyfriends."

It was not a direct question and Rynn had shown she would speak only when the man made his demands unmistakable. Instead of pressing her, Hallet shifted the question to the boy.

"You her boyfriend?"

"Yes."

Hallet turned his face, fiery red, to the girl.

"You said 'no boyfriends.'" The man included the table with its two plates in his gaze. "Looks to me like you even entertain your boyfriends at dinner parties. With candlelight and wine."

Suddenly Hallet faced Mario. "She's very young. How old did she tell you she was?"

"Thirteen."

"Fourteen, thirteen—younger than you, right?"

Mario nodded.

"Don't you know any girls your own age? Or do girls your own age like to dance?"

"The jelly glasses," the girl said boldly.

"Yes?"

"On the telephone we talked about the jelly glasses. They're ready for you to take."

"Not now."

Rynn weighed the man's every word. Did he mean he was not going now and therefore the glasses could wait, or did he mean that now his mother would never again have use of them? She did not need to study the red face at the fire to know he was enjoying this intentional ambiguity. Her father had had a friend in London, a barrister, a man who loved the maze of the law and the labyrinth he could make of half-answers every bit as much as her father loved working always to be precise and make his meaning exact and clear.

"Perhaps Dear Mother came by but you weren't home."

"I was here all the time."

"Didn't go to the football game?"

"No."

"On Saturday afternoons this time of year everyone goes to the football game. Today the Wildcats won." Hallet was looking at Mario. "Did you know that?"

"Yes."

"Hardly a soul in the village this afternoon." He was still looking at Mario. "Right?"

But Mario was looking at Rynn.

"You go to the football game?" Hallet asked.

"No."

"You play football?"

Before Mario could answer, Rynn said, "I couldn't possibly have missed her."

Hallet spoke only to Mario, "I didn't hear you answer."

"No. I don't play football."

"I don't play football either. Saturday afternoons I listen to the Metropolitan Opera. On the radio. In the office. But I see you get all dressed up—"

"He does a magic show," said Rynn.

"That makes two of us in the village who don't play football." The man looked again at Rynn. "You said you were here all the time?"

"Yes."

"Couldn't have missed her?"

"No."

"Strange."

"You can take them for her now," the girl said.

"The jelly glasses?"

"I can put them in your car," said Mario.

"Can you?"

"I'll do it now."

"You can't."

There it was again. The maddening ambiguity Hallet led them into, the subtle little confusions.

"I don't mind," the boy said, by which he meant that he was both able and willing to take the glasses out of the house. He would do it now.

"I said you can't." The man snapped his fingers at the cigarette box which Mario brought to him. Mario returned the box to the table and struck a match to carry the flame to light the cigarette. Hallet breathed deeply. To Rynn he seemed not so much to exhale as to allow the smoke to leak out of him, blue curls of smoke that hung around his puffy red face.

"Can't," the man said. "No car. I walked here tonight. My

dear wife has the station wagon. Mother's very grand and liver-colored Bentley sits majestically in front of the office." He drew smoke from the cigarette. "Dear Mother has the keys."

Rynn told herself that her eyes must not seek Mario's. Hallet appeared content to gaze, to ponder the mystery of his burning cigarette.

A spark snapped out of the fireplace and lay glowing on the hearth. Then it died.

Around the house the autumn wind moaned. Tree branches clashed.

Time after time Rynn tried to break the silence till she had begun to doubt she was capable of uttering a word. When she finally began she prayed her voice would not screech out all the panic that churned inside.

"It's very late, Mr. Hallet. I'll have to ask you to excuse us now."

To her surprise the words came out clearly, even calmly. When the man gave no indication he had heard what she said, though of course he had, she felt she must not lose the confidence her first words had given her, but thrust on.

"What do you want, Mr. Hallet?"

The man smoked. He glanced over his shoulder at the boy, who still stood leaning on his cane.

"What do *you* want?"

"What do you mean?" Mario's voice was another croak.

"I mean exactly what I'm asking. What do you want?"

"Does everybody have to want something?"

Hallet's pink fingers brought the Gauloise to his shiny lips. "Of course. Right now we're waiting. We're waiting to hear what *you* want."

"I'm waiting too." The boy fought to struggle out the words.

"Then we'll all wait together." Hallet allowed the silence

to return. One of those deafening silences, it had a presence that could almost be felt, like water soundlessly filling a vault. In time this kind of silence could kill.

"I'd say you want what all boyfriends want." Hallet smoked. "Is that what you want?"

"No."

Eyebrows slowly climbed on Hallet's shiny red brow.

"You don't like girls?"

"Yes, but . . ."

"Then you don't want Rynn?"

Rynn ached to break into this cross-examination, to help the boy, but she knew Hallet would ignore her. Or worse. The man would take anything she might say in an effort to help Mario and twist it around, and trap her deeper in his maze.

"Little magician," Hallet said, "why don't you do a trick we'll all like? Disappear yourself?"

Rynn found Hallet's eyes glittering at her.

"Tell him to go home."

"He's my friend."

"But not your boyfriend?"

Vastly pleased with himself, Hallet sucked in cigarette smoke. Slowly he sent it out in a thin blue stream. With his cigarette he indicated the girl.

"Shall I tell you what *you* want?"

Rynn could not bring herself to raise her eyes to the man.

"We'll save that," he said. "First, I shall tell you what I want."

Hallet rose and came to the fireplace to stand over Rynn where she sat on the woodbox.

"I want to know what's happening. Here—in this house. I want to know what's *been* happening. What happened today."

"Nothing happened," the girl managed to say.

Hallet looked down at her, almost as a teacher might stand over a student. His tone was as patronizing as a teacher's, a tone calculated to put everything the child said into doubt.

"All day is a long time for nothing to happen."

Rynn shook her head. "Nothing."

Still the instructor, still playing the role of one on the road to truth, he was deliberately slowing down the review of facts so no point would escape either student or teacher.

"Just now. The police were here. *That* happened."

Rynn shook her head, but the adult would not allow his pupil to retreat into silence.

"Police. Here. Yes or no?"

Rynn nodded.

"*Yes or no?*"

"Officer Miglioriti said you called him. He said you were worried about your mother."

"Yes?" His one word was an order to keep talking.

"He said that you thought . . ."

"Yes?"

"He said that you thought if you could learn where your mother had been . . ."

"Been? Since when?"

"Since she left her office."

"Good." Hallet sat on the woodbox beside the girl, who held her breath.

"Then what did the officer think I'd think?"

"If you could find where your mother had been, you'd learn where your mother is."

"Do you think the officer's right?"

Rynn tried to shrug. The heavy smell of cologne almost made her gag.

"Yes or no?"

"Yes."

Hallet smoked.

"That's *part* of what I want."

"There are the glasses."

Hallet did not need to glance at the carton against the wall. They were already as much a presence in the room as any one of them.

"So they are."

"Waiting for her."

"Meaning?"

"She hasn't been here."

"Wrong. We're going too fast." His tone was professorial again. "I'll have to correct your logic. All those glasses sitting there proves—what? That those glasses are still sitting there."

"Then I'm afraid I can't help you."

"You want to help?"

The girl twisted her face from the cologne and cigarette smoke.

"Yes."

"Then what do you suggest we do?"

"We call the police."

"Already did. Seems we need *more* help." Hallet's gaze moved to Mario: "Do *you* want to help?"

"Yes."

"Then go ask her father to help us."

The boy gulped and stammered. "He's sleeping."

"In the next room?"

"Yes," the boy nodded vigorously.

Hallet spoke to Rynn. "In the hall. That's his study?"

She nodded.

"He sleeps there, too?" Hallet rose.

"I promised not to wake him," said the girl.

Hallet was moving toward the door in the hall.

"Let's wake him up and ask him if he can help us find Dear Mother."

Slowly he took another step as if he expected the girl to try to stop him.

"This room—you're sure?"

Mario, his black cape flying, lurched to the hall and stumbled past Hallet to block his way to the door.

"Rynn, pick up the phone!"

At the phone the girl saw Hallet advance, looming over the boy. Dropping the cat-and-mouse game, he glared at him.

"I told you to get out!"

Mario, not daring to look at him, as if Hallet's answering eyes would make him falter, shook his head.

"*You and your wop tricks, get the hell out!*"

"Rynn—go! Run to the neighbors!"

The girl dropped the phone onto the hook, ran to the hall, but slowed as she assessed her chances of dashing past Hallet.

"Go ahead," said Hallet. "Run."

"*Run!*" Mario was begging her.

Hallet made no move to block the front door. Suddenly his smile, outlined with the balm's shine, glinted in the shadows.

"Run where?" His hand indicated she was free to open the door.

"Your neighbors aren't even home. The Jews all went to Florida."

"Call the police!" Mario yelled.

Hallet strode to the kitchen counter and grabbed the receiver from the hook. He made the line into a loop around his fist.

"Do I pull this out?"

"If you do that they'll know it's out of order," said the girl. "Who's going to call at this time of night?"

"*Put it down!*" The order came from Mario—a surprise to

both Hallet and Rynn, for the boy seemed to blaze with a dangerous energy that neither had suspected lay coiled beneath the sweet smile. He pulled abruptly at his cane, which clicked apart to open in half. From the sheath he drew out a long, shining blade.

Hallet, staring at the sword, rattled the telephone receiver back on the counter.

Mario, his fury uncoiled, lurched without his cane toward the man, the sword in his tensed fist. "I'm a wop. Wops carry knives. Right?"

Hallet fell back from the limping boy, and twisted himself away from the counter toward the door. A pink hand signaled for a truce.

"Keep away!" Hallet's voice exploded in a piercing shriek charged with fury and rage.

"Guinea? Dago? Wop?" The ferocious boy struggled toward the man.

Hallet wheeled around to prevent his attacker from outmaneuvering him. Falling back again, he barked out what he hoped sounded like a laugh. "It's a trick! A trick cane!"

"Is it?" with another step Mario dragged himself closer.

Hallet's pink face trickled sweat. He backed into the hall.

The boy jabbed the sword out in front of him.

Hallet crashed into the bicycle, regained his balance and flung open the front door. He was gone.

Rynn rushed for the door, slammed it shut and hurled herself against it. She looked to Mario who was signaling for absolute silence. She nodded, only too relieved to say nothing, too exhausted to do anything but fall against the door.

Mario picked up the other half of the cane and fitted the stick back together. "Call the police," he said.

In the dark hall Rynn leaned against the door.

"We don't dare."

A sudden thought hurried the boy across the parlor toward the woodbox. Only as he was about to lift the lid did he realize Rynn had run past him.

She sat on the box.

"You didn't want him to look in here, did you?"

A toss of the girl's head threw her long hair out of her eyes.

"You don't want me to ask why it's there."

He pushed the girl, but it was not his force that made her move. She stepped away from the box and allowed him to lift the heavy cover. Reaching down among the maple logs he lifted out the umbrella.

He snapped it open.

"Hers?"

Rynn reached for the umbrella, closed it with a snap, and tossed it onto the couch, then crossed the oak floor to the table where she waited, signaling him with a glance to join her. She motioned for him to pick up his side of the table.

The two moved the gateleg table off the braided rug.

With her bare feet Rynn rolled the rug back. She knelt at the hasp and pushed back the bolt. With one hand she lifted the door till it stood perpendicular; then she let it fall back against the wall.

She rose and moved to the front of the trap, to stand at the top of the stairs. She motioned for Mario to take the pewter candlestick, light the candle, and follow her.

Mario carried the flame to the girl, who peered down the stairs. Motionless, she waited for the boy to take the first step.

She could feel Mario hesitate. She knew his every instinct was telling him to turn back, go, leave, run anywhere to keep from walking down those stairs into the dark.

Across the candle's wavering flame, he looked at Rynn. Their eyes met for only a second. His faltered.

Rynn was waiting for the boy to walk down the stairs.

At last Mario took his first step.

Rynn followed.

13

"THAT'S TO WARM IT," the girl said as Mario watched her pour boiling water into a teapot.

"We don't drink too much tea at our place."

"If you'll put the biscuits on a plate, they can go on the tray with the tea things."

The boy arranged the cookies into two rings on the plate, examined his work and seemed satisfied.

"Rynn?"

"Mm?"

"How long for your mother?"

The girl poured the steaming water from the teapot into the sink.

"October seventeenth."

"Wow," the boy said. He watched her drop a few pinches of loose tea into the pot.

"But, I mean, don't bodies . . ."

From the kettle the girl poured the boiling water in with the tea leaves.

"Decompose?"

Mario, who found himself unable to say the word, nodded his head.

From the cupboard Rynn took the tea things and asked him to put them on a tray. He did as she said, but he was waiting to hear her explain how to keep a body from decomposing.

"You can put stuff on them," she said, opening the refrigerator and taking out a carton of milk.

"Yeah?"

She filled a little creamer and handed it to him.

"Wow," he said. "But how did you know how to do that?"

"The tray's ready now, if you want to take it to the fireplace."

"Okay." He was grateful she did not ask him if he could manage the tray along with his cane, and he held it with great care as the girl took two teaspoons from a drawer.

"Rynn?"

She left the kitchen area and ran to clear a place for the tray on the coffee table. Holding the tray level to compensate for his limp, Mario brought it in front of the fire where she waited.

"How did I know how to do that to a body? Is that what you want to know?"

The boy, holding the tea tray, did not reply.

"I told you. It's exactly the same as cooking. I happen to know how to read."

"The library has stuff on things like that?"

The girl picked up the poker and pushed a maple log back into the fire. "The library has everything."

"Wow. I guess."

Mario put the tray on the table. From the floor he picked up Mrs. Hallet's candy-stripe umbrella.

"We'll have to get rid of this too."

Rynn seemed preoccupied with the fire.

"Did you notice?" he asked, "I said *we*."

"I noticed. Thank you."

"He'll be back. Hallet I mean."

"I know."

"I'll help you."

She dropped the poker into the open woodbox. The boy held the umbrella.

"Of course you have a right to know what happened."

Seating herself effortlessly on the floor beside the coffee table she seemed to Mario to move as gracefully as a dancer in her long white caftan. She drew her bare feet under her legs. Mario steadied himself, one hand on the table, to sit on the floor across from her. Reaching inside the blue embroidery at the neck of her dress, Rynn drew out a folded letter which she handed to him.

By the light of the fire he saw the black ink and bold handwriting on gray stationery, a letter Rynn's father had written to her their last night in London.

As he read, the girl arranged two cups, put a strainer across one, lifted the teapot and carefully began to pour.

Mario read the letter twice then refolded it, and because he felt he must not put it down on the table, that he must not put it anywhere but back into Rynn's hands, he held it.

"In London my father'd been taking treatments for what we thought was a stomach ulcer. One evening—spring—when it stayed daylight very late into the evening, one of those evenings birds were still chirping, we walked to what had been—before he became ill—our favorite restaurant. Indian. Father ordered curry. A man with a stomach ulcer? One of those terribly hot curries. I stared at him. He leaned across the table, kissed me, and said it didn't matter any more."

She had poured both cups of tea.

"Milk and sugar?"

Mario nodded. The girl's motions were practiced. Two tiny spoonfuls of sugar went into his tea. She poured exactly the amount of milk to fill the cup, cutting its flow off with a snap of the wrist so expertly that not one drop spilled. She handed him the saucer.

He held it, the cup chattering against the saucer.

She put only a pinch of sugar into her cup, lifted it delicately, but instead of sipping, she took her teaspoon and stirred the tea.

"After my father and I finished that dinner, we walked and walked in the soft London night. We planned together —very carefully—what we must do—once my father was dead—to keep my mother who'd been living in Italy from swooping down on me."

The boy's cup and saucer rattled and he returned it to the table. The girl took the letter and put it inside her caftan.

"When I say the word *mother* it doesn't mean a thing. My only memory of her is her bright-red fingernails. She'd run off years ago. Which was actually a very good thing as she had once been arrested for beating me. One day my father came home, found her bashing about the house in a drunken stupor, me black-and-blue, and on the spot, he kicked her out and raised me. I only saw the woman one time before she came here. That was the time my father won a prize for his poetry and she smelled money. Other than that he only had a bit of money, you see. Not a lot, but enough that once he was gone, we could count on her flapping down and sinking her great painted claws into me."

She offered the boy the plate with the cookies.

"Biscuits?"

The boy took one with slivered almonds on top.

"*I* would have gone to a lawyer."

"No you wouldn't."

Her harshness surprised him.

"Why use up all the money on lawyers and then have to do what the court says. All that would do is make the court

decide how I'd be reared, which means what school they'd
lock me up in."

"You should have got a guardian."

"A godfather?"

"I'm serious."

"Who? My father didn't have any living relatives. The
only people we knew were mad poets. The poets we knew—
except for my father—may be madly talented, but they
wouldn't make very good parents."

"Besides, you don't need anybody you're so staggeringly
brilliant."

She looked at Mario. He shrugged. "That was supposed
to be a joke."

"It happens to be true. That's why my father sold off
everything, got all the money he could and left England
without a word to anyone. That was last spring. All spring
and summer we drove a rented car from North Carolina
and the place where Carl Sandburg lived, to Maine to find
the place I liked best."

"Then you found this?"

"Do you have to fool with that umbrella?"

Mario looked down. He was holding the umbrella in the
same way he sometimes held his cane, as a wand.

"Sorry."

From where he sat he opened the lid of the woodbox
and tossed the umbrella inside. He lowered the lid.

"That was just after Labor Day. People were packing up
and streaming back into the city. We came down this lane
with the dense trees that seemed to be reaching out and
touching hands overhead. Then I saw the yard full of zinnias
blazing with color. We got out of the car and looked
through the window. One could see no one lived here. My
father asked me if I was quite certain I could spend the next
three years of my life here exactly as we planned it. He

wouldn't let me decide for a week. He made me think about it very carefully after we had found out through the estate agents in the village, that it was free. He leased the house . . . paid for it for the next three years."

She lifted her tea and stirred it with a spoon but did not sip.

"Good tea," said Mario.

"Good," she said. "We'll make an Englishman out of you yet."

They glanced at each other. Again something had been said that included them in a future together.

"Almost all of September my father looked fine, and if the pain was terrible he never said a thing. He'd go into that room, close the door, take something. Right up till the last we'd go for long walks, through the lanes, along the beach. For miles and miles and miles. One Sunday evening when it was very hot and breathlessly still we were sitting here in this room in the dusk. He switched on the record player. Liszt. We sat. As I say, here. In this very room. We listened to the piece. Neither of us said a word. That's when he took my hand and we went out into the garden. In a quiet voice he said that I wasn't like any other person in the world and that some people wouldn't understand that. They wouldn't want me to be the way I was. They'd want to change me. They'd try to order me about and make me into the kind of person they wanted me to be. Since I was still a child there would be little I could do except stay alone, stay out of trouble, and make myself very small in the world."

"Alone?" Mario spoke the word as if it were only a concept, something he could not quite imagine, certainly not a way of life.

"We'd worked out every detail of it," she said. "We both knew full well it wouldn't be easy. 'Do anything you must,' father said. 'Fight them any way you have to. *Survive*.' He kissed me—it was in the grape arbor—and then he walked off through the trees and down the lane."

"He never came back?" Mario went deep red, showing immediately that he wished to hell he had not said those words. Of course he knew her father had never come back.

"In that room—on his desk—I found charts—tide-tables of the waters both in the Sound and the ocean. What he'd been doing was studying the tides. He'll never be found."

"Did you cry a lot?"

"Depends on what you mean by a lot. No, I don't think so."

"You believe in God?"

"It would be nice."

"But you don't."

"I don't know."

"Me too."

He crunched another cookie and washed it down with a gulp of tea.

"You shouldn't keep money around the house," he said.

"My father and I opened a joint checking account. I have absolutely heaps of traveler's checks."

"Can kids have them?"

Her gaze was steady across her teacup. "I just told you I do."

She reached down inside her caftan where she had put the letter. This time she pulled out a gold chain and dangled a key. She almost smiled as she gave the key a swing and it described a circle. "I keep most of them in a safe deposit box at the bank."

"I never heard of a kid having traveler's checks before."

"I said 'heaps,' but actually I have to make them last three years." She dropped the key and the chain back down inside her gown.

"So now you know," she said.

"Yeah," he was staring at his tea.

"Rynn?"

"Mm?"

"Would it be so awful, I mean, if you did have to play the game?"

"But that's what this has been all for—"

"I know," he said. "No, I don't really. Maybe what I don't understand is what you and your father mean by the game."

She sighed deeply as if to say he was not trying to understand.

"The game is pretending. It's going through the motions of life. But it's not *living*."

"School's living."

"No." Rynn shook her head till she had to brush her long hair away from her eyes. "School is having people tell you what living is, not finding out for yourself."

"But you have to go to school."

"Why?"

"To learn something."

"Such as?"

"Read and write. And—"

"I can't read? I can't write?"

"Okay. So your father taught you. What if a person doesn't have a father like yours?"

"Did I ever say I was talking about anyone but myself? If you love school so much good luck to you."

"Except I don't think you mean that."

"Why should I want everyone to be like me any more than I want to be like everyone else?"

"*I'm* not like everyone else," Mario protested.

"I'm talking about *them*."

"Who?"

"All of them with their bubble gum and trashy music and football games."

"It's not all like that—"

"School is for kids who will grow up and never write a poem or sing a song or *do* anything." Her faith in what she was saying was complete. "Like doing a magic trick. Did school teach you to do magic?"

"No."

"You see?" She folded her arms across her white caftan. "The game is for people who want rules because they're afraid to believe anything everyone else doesn't already believe. They're all scared to leave the street where they live and *do* something with their lives. The game is for people who want to be *told* what to do. Okay. Good for them, if that's what they want."

"Everyone can't be like you."

"Nobody's like anybody! I just told you, nobody else has to live the way I do."

"Living like this . . . wow! I mean . . ."

"Yes?" There was that harshness again, a challenge.

"I mean people *help* people."

"You've got a family."

"*Other* people. They want to. Sometimes," he added weakly.

"In my case there was no one. Are you saying that my father and I didn't think long and hard about it? Do you imagine we just decided this overnight? I mean for me it would have meant some hideous school smelling of chalk and cabbage—"

"You might have found a good school."

"A school! A school telling me how to live, what to think, what to do with the rest of my life. A school with my money managed by some solicitor until *they* decided I was old enough to be trusted with what was mine. Besides . . ."

She stirred her tea. "This is only the way I live now. I only have to be careful till they *think* I'm old enough to do as I choose."

"Who's they?"

"Everyone!"

"Wow. You know how that sounds? I mean you keep saying *they*—like everyone's out to get you."

"Maybe they are."

The boy gulped his tea before he said, "You've got to trust *someone!*"

Suddenly, Mario found he could not meet Rynn's eyes. Nor could she bear to look directly at him, as if only now, only after she had told him things she had told no one else, both of them had begun to fathom what she, what they, had done.

Mario studied the tea she had not touched.

"How did she—your mother—find you?"

Rynn put the saucer on the coffee table and stared into the fire. "My fault actually. A poem I published. My first feelings about this place. Friends of hers saw it in England and sent it on to her in Greece. People who know Long Island recognized places I wrote about. One day a taxi stopped out there in the lane. . . ."

Mario wondered if she intended to go on. Perhaps he had heard all she was willing to share. He felt that asking her to reveal more might make her retreat into silence. But she did speak.

"The front door was open. She walked right in—fingernails as red as ever. I loathed myself for doing it, but I actually pretended to be happy to see her. My God, the nerve of her, coming here. . . . She was the kind of woman who thinks everyone will forgive her anything. She sat right in that chair, smoked her gold-tipped cigarettes and went on and on about how awful the pollution in the Mediterra-

nean was getting to be, and how much she loathed and
detested the Greeks, how marvelous it would be to live
here."

Rynn turned from the fire to look beyond Mario at the
rocking chair.

"We had tea then as well. She wanted a drink but I didn't
have any. Tea. And the same almond biscuits."

"They're very good."

"She liked them too."

The boy took another cookie. It did taste strongly of almonds. After a moment, he asked,

"*In* the tea?"

She nodded.

Mario, who was sipping at this moment, suddenly stopped
and he wondered if he could swallow.

"Potassium cyanide."

The boy was trying to keep his cup from chattering in the
saucer.

"The Wilsons used the studio as a darkroom. I found
the stuff when my father and I packed away their photo-
graphic chemicals. As I said before, I can read. I read the
warning on the label."

The girl's tea glinted in the firelight. She had not taken
one sip from the cup. Her eyes met his. Very calmly she
said, "It's too hot. I didn't put any cold milk in mine."

Mario wondered if she could see that he was beginning to
sweat.

But she was thinking of her mother.

"I can still see her red nails holding the cup. After a few
sips she said her tea tasted of almonds."

Mario's cup clattered until the saucer was safely on the
table.

"Of course it tasted of almonds." The girl swung her hair
back from her eyes. "You know what I told her?"

Mario's face gleamed in the firelight. He felt his shirt, streaming wet under the armpits, its back drenched and sticking to him.

"It's the almond biscuit, I told her. She believed that. They come from Fortnum's, I said. 'Lovely,' she said. And she did—she really loved that. She loved anything that came from the posh shops. She'd put better labels into coats, and she'd only carry the poshest shopping bags. Harrods, at the very least." Rynn was in her own world, talking to herself.

Mario felt his throat tighten. He was terribly aware of each breath he took. Each was more of a struggle.

"How long did it take?" he managed to ask.

"Quite fast actually."

"Like first you get sleepy?"

"Apparently. Very."

Mario's hand sought the floor. It was steady. He felt feverish; he was sweating. Each breath took increasing effort.

Rynn's untouched cup of tea shimmered in front of him.

"You tired?"

Mario shook his head to deny the weariness he fought.

"No." His voice was a rasp.

"I shouldn't wonder if you were," Rynn said. "It's late." Her hand sought his, but he pulled away.

"Do you know what I think might be a very good idea? I think it might be a very good idea if you were to ring your parents. Tell them you're still at the birthday party."

"But I'm not—" He coughed.

"But earlier you told your mother you were."

Mario was shaking his head. He did not want to call.

"I really do. I think you should ring your family. Want me to bring the phone to you?"

"What good would that do you?"

"*Us,*" she corrected him.

"My Uncle Ron knows I'm here."

"He won't tell. Ring them. Tell them you're still at the party."

He shook his head no.

"Then what happened. I mean to her." Somehow Mario fought his way through this thicket of words, the confusion, the web in which he was convinced she was trying to ensnare him.

"Mother struggled to catch her breath."

"And then?"

"Then? Finally she just . . . slumped over. In that chair."

Mario's mind raced. He would telephone. He would tell the girl he was telephoning his family, but instead he would call the hospital and have them send an ambulance.

"She lay in that chair a very long time whilst I wondered what to do with her. I didn't think of the trapdoor to the cellar. Not then. As you say about magic, one doesn't think to do the obvious. Not at first."

He saw her pick up the teapot.

"More?"

Weak with dread he made a sign that meant no.

"I guess I will phone."

"Good." The girl rose. "You wait here, I'll bring it to you." She ran barefoot across the shining floor.

She put the phone beside him.

"You *are* tired."

Mario forced himself to sit up.

"Do you want me to dial it for you?"

So that's her plan. She knows I'll call for help, so she's not going to let me call anyone but them, and that's to set up her alibi. . . . *What can I do? Can I grab the phone and call the hospital?* . . .

"Are you all right?"

"I'm okay," he managed to whisper.

What can I do? . . .

His mind raced; he considered running from the house. On his goddamn cane. How far could he hope to get— Suddenly the girl's hand reached out and her move stopped any further thoughts of escape. He could only stare.

She had lifted her saucer and was sipping her tea. With her other white hand she had picked up an almond cookie which she nibbled. A pink tongue, like a kitten's, ran over her lips collecting stray crumbs.

"Listen," she said, but this time there was no urgency in her command.

Mario strained to hear what had drawn her attention.

"The wind," the boy said.

"Creatures chuckling on the roofs and whistling in the air."

Again Rynn reached for his hand. This time he did not pull away. She spoke and Mario wondered if the lines were her father's poetry.

> An awful Tempest mashed the air—
> The clouds were gaunt, and few—
> A black—as of a Spectre's Cloak
> Hid Heaven and Earth from view.
>
> The creatures chuckled on the Roofs—
> And whistled in the air—
> And shook their fists—
> And gnashed their teeth—
> And swung their frenzied hair.

Rynn rose and took the tray noiselessly into the kitchen.

With both hands on the table, Mario found he was able to stand.

"And swung their frenzied hair. Wow!"

"Does that give you a chill?"

"Like sandpaper up and down your back when it gets really good in opera."

Mario waited till her back was turned to rise. On his feet and assured that he was still alive, he broke into his beautiful sunshine grin.

The girl rinsed out the teacups and put them on the counter to drain. She was drying the teapot.

Mario stretched his arms till he felt the muscles in his young body ache pleasantly and his blood surge through his limbs. He twisted, enjoying the warming feeling.

When Rynn, teapot in hand, turned to face him, he suddenly dropped his arms and stood motionless. Even though an immense surge of relief flooded him, and in spite of all the love he felt for this girl, he dared show nothing. He had to mask his sudden joy, or the abrupt change would betray all the doubts he had suffered till only a moment ago.

"Your father write that?"

"Emily Dickinson."

"Got anything she's written?"

"I know most of it by heart."

Mario went to the rocking chair.

Rynn watched the boy sit. Slowly she moved across the room to the chair and sank to the floor beside him. She leaned her head against his knee. His hand sought her shining brown hair. Her hand covered his.

14

A WEEK PASSED.

Mario could not come to Rynn on Sunday, for Sunday as he explained, meant Mass in the morning, a family dinner of almost tribal proportions, and visits with countless relatives. But he came twice during the week.

On Monday he reported that the liver-colored Bentley had been towed, still locked, into his father's garage. Everyone in town knew Mrs. Hallet was missing. At the service station and on the streets the year-round residents had begun to greet each other with a demand for news. As no facts were available, they supplied each other with rumors. These, Mario announced, only proved how much people hated the Hallets.

On Thursday he reviewed the week that had begun with most of the village saying that Frank Hallet's wife had taken her children and left him. For the neighbors, the defection was the evidence they had waited for. Did that not prove Hallet had something to do with his mother's disappearance? By midweek everyone had agreed that Frank Hallet had always hated his mother. At the garage, Mario's father was able to corroborate this assertion by reminding each local customer who stopped for gas, oil, or a tune-up that relations had always been strained between mother and son. After all, the woman had always refused to allow her son to drive the now legendary liver-colored Bentley.

No one but Mario came to the house in the lane.

More precisely, no one came to the door. During the night Rynn had seen a spotlight from a police car sweep the house. Officer Miglioriti was keeping an eye on the place.

Rynn was careful to lock the doors and windows, and she left the light burning in front of the house every night. If anyone—and she could not bring herself to think of that someone as Hallet—if anyone had passed the front window, she had seen no shadow on the curtains.

During school hours she did not appear on the streets of the village out of fear some adult would stop her and ask her why she was not in class. After school, when students wandered freely, she dared not leave the house in case she would miss Mario.

On the chance the telephone was tapped, they did not call one another.

This Saturday, like the last, Mario brought his bicycle into the hall, but not because of the rain. The day, so far, was cold and clear, but they agreed there was no sense in leaving it outside to show anyone who came down the lane that the boy was in the house.

What a wonderful day it was to get into the outdoors. The sky above the tree branches was blue, dappled by fast-running clouds shifting the autumn sunlight between sharp spangles of yellow light and an amber haze.

Though Rynn realized it was painful for Mario to walk, she was grateful that he was at her side, hand in hand, and they wandered for more than two hours through the lane and along the beach, where a surf, gray as lead, unfolded.

Under the wide sky the stretch of sand was empty except for a few gulls that waited until the two were almost upon them before they flapped, screeched, and sailed off on the wind.

Alone on the beach, Rynn led Mario to the damp sand where the breakers fanned out and vanished under their feet. She put something into his hand.

Mario did not need to look to know he held Mrs. Hallet's keys. The girl told him he could throw farther than she.

When the keys had disappeared into the sea, they walked on in silence. Neither spoke of the work that lay ahead.

During the week they had planned every detail of what they must do. Now they were waiting till the football game began in town. Frank Hallet had said it, and Mario had agreed it was true: On Saturday everyone goes to the football game.

At one o'clock when the game began, they went into the grape arbor, which they explored in silence. Then Rynn posted herself at the side of the house, a sentinel on guard against anyone who might approach up or down the lane.

Mario raked the leaves from the patch of yard beyond the arbor and began to dig. The soil of the old garden, worked by so many generations, was free of stones and tangled roots and yielded to the spade. At the end of an hour the girl, leaning in her duffle coat against a chestnut tree watching Mario work, listening to his spade clink on the occasional stone, saw only his head and shoulders above the pit.

When the hole was even deeper, they returned to the house where Rynn drew the front curtains tight.

"Okay?" asked Mario.

Rynn nodded, the signal to begin.

Together they lifted the table to one side, rolled the

braided rug, and pulled back the trapdoor till it leaned against the wall.

As Rynn ran to the kitchen for two boxes of Saran Wrap, Mario opened the window to the grape arbor. At another nod from Rynn, he led the way down into the cellar.

Only a plan that had been worked out in detail could have allowed them to act so quickly. They struggled up the cellar stairs with the first of their wrapped burdens.

"Careful," whispered Rynn. "Don't get any of that chemical stuff on you."

"Rest it on the window sill," Mario grunted. "Okay. Now we both push."

They were carrying their second burden from the cellar when a car horn honked.

Their hearts stopped.

"It's out in the lane," whispered Mario. "What if they're coming here?"

For an instant Rynn searched Mario's face before she motioned toward the open window.

"We have to get it out! Fast!"

As Mario clambered over the sill to follow the second bundle into the grape arbor, Rynn closed the windows, pulled the curtains, and raced to the front window to peer into the road. After more than a minute she left the front door to go into the yard where she could look down the lane. Then she hurried through the leaves around the corner of the house to report to Mario that a white dog had ambled in front of a car.

In the same way they had worked together inside, the two carried the wrapped bundles to the pit.

Mario grabbed the shovel and dug the earth; Rynn, at the corner of the house, felt a cold tingle of mist on her face as she huddled down where she could see both the back-yard and the lane through the trees.

She listened to the earth from Mario's spade thud into the pit and shivered as her eyes searched the gray clouds which thickened and filled the sky. A fine rain was already glinting on the leaves and branches.

When the gentle rain grew heavy, Rynn left her post long enough to bring her father's macintosh from the house, only to find that Mario's wool pullover and Levis were already sodden. His black hair was flat and wet on his head and water streamed down his frowning face. The fresh-turned earth was melting into slippery mud, an ooze that was heavy on the shovel, but the boy worked without stopping.

Rynn dashed back inside and heated a can of cream of celery soup, which she carried in a cup through a driving rain.

Mario paused only long enough to gulp the steaming soup.

"Go back in." His teeth chattered on the cup. "There's no sense in both of us getting soaked."

Rynn took the empty cup that still warmed her hands and returned to her guard post. Soon the cup was cold and she pulled the damp coat that smelled of wet wool up to her ears. She wondered how long she would be able to bear shaking with cold, waiting here in the rain. At least Mario was digging and that kept him moving. Determined not to leave him and her post, she retreated only far enough to seek the protection of an overhanging eave where water from a broken downspout gushed at her feet.

As minutes dragged by and she pushed strands of dripping hair back from her face, she was more and more tempted to do as he had insisted, to run into the house, strip off the wet coat and build the fire into a warming blaze.

"Hi!"

Rynn tensed.

Someone was calling through the rain. She dared not

even breathe. She took care to look slowly, so as not to give away her surprise, in the direction of the voice. There, between the tree trunks near the road, was a man walking toward her, a man walking toward the backyard.

Should she call out to Mario? What could he do?

Rynn dodged past the downspout and hurried toward the stranger.

Halfway to the road she slowed her steps. The man wore a bright red parka that covered his head. With black rubber boots he looked like a tall, thin Santa Claus coming at her through the tree trunks.

Rynn's mind raced for something to call out, something to do, some way to keep the man from approaching the house. On impulse she raced forward to meet him.

"You seen my dog?"

From where he stood Rynn was sure the man could not see into the backyard, but she feared he might still hear Mario's shovel working the wet earth.

"My dog," he called. "I'm looking for my dog."

"What kind of dog?" Rynn forced her voice into a monotone in an effort to cover her panic.

"English pit bull."

"White?"

"You've seen him?"

The man was about to come closer, but she nodded and pointed down the lane and away from the house. "Out there."

He stopped.

"About ten minutes ago."

"Thanks." The man turned, but he made no move.

Go!

What did he want now?

"You better get inside." His voice was a white mist. "Out here you'll get wet."

Rynn watched his red parka move through the trees till he reached the road. Not until he was out of sight did she stumble back toward the corner of the house. Before she reached the grape arbor she heard the slap of the shovel on mud.

She shrank back under the eave to watch Mario work.

When, at last, the boy flattened the gobs of mud with the back of his shovel and began to rake wet leaves back over the wounded earth, Rynn ran into the house.

By the time he finished in the garden she was standing at the back window holding a huge bath towel.

"Throw the shovel under the porch."

Mud-spattered, his wet clothes clinging to him, Mario evoked in Rynn that same squeeze of the heart she had felt seeing a puppy, plump and fluffy, miserably wet and shivering. He was that thin and vulnerable.

The boy did not do as she ordered. Instead, he hurled the shovel into the dense tangle of underbrush at the back of the garden. This was not part of the plan and his thought was better than hers.

Rynn pulled Mario in the front door, turning quickly to slam and lock it. As he tugged off his muddy boots, she covered his dripping black hair with the towel.

"You're soaked through!"

She began to rub his hair vigorously with the towel. "We have to get you warm and dry. *Hurry!*"

When he reached out to his bicycle for support, she nudged her shoulder under his arm. Bearing much of his weight, she moved him through the hall.

He coughed.

She urged Mario to dry his hair, backed him toward the stairs, and pushed him down to sit as she pulled off his wet socks.

"You were right about doing it on Saturday," she said

unpeeling the wet wool, rolling it down over his ankles and across his feet. "Everyone *was* at the football game."

He sucked his breath in over chattering teeth, incapable of speech, his entire body quaking.

"Just as soon as we get you out of the rest of these wet things I've got a hot tub waiting upstairs. *Hurry.*" She tugged at his pullover, heavy and wet. She unbuttoned a cold wet shirt, stripping it from his shivering white shoulders.

"Out there, I should have helped you."

She unbuckled his belt. His shaking hands, blue with cold, fumbled, but worked the zipper and undid the fly so she could draw off his trousers. From under the towel, a tent over his head, she found his black eyes watching her, and felt a stab of guilt: He knew exactly what she was thinking, and as she pulled off his trousers, she made a point of not looking at his legs to see if they were crippled. Both legs, as far as she could tell, looked the same, both equally white and hairless; both shook with cold.

"Like letting someone look at your chipped tooth," he said.

She pulled him to her and wrapped the towel around him.

"Come on."

But after a single step, she froze. He lifted the towel from his head.

"Hear something?"

"No."

"What is it?"

"Nothing," she said, but she was shaking.

"Don't worry so much. The rain's not going to wash away all that dirt in the back garden." His arm went around her. Now it was he who was helping her up the stairs.

"Come on. And don't worry. I dug plenty deep."

Rynn tensed and stood motionless. Something even worse

than the worry of the earth washing away from what had been in the cellar gripped her.

She could barely bring herself to speak the words.

"Her umbrella. We forgot her umb—"

"It's *with* her."

From the bathroom upstairs they heard the telephone on the kitchen counter shrill again and again, long past the time when most callers would have given up. Rynn, drying her arms with a towel, raced down the stairs and clutched the instrument.

"Yes?"

She had not missed the call, but whoever was on the line said nothing. Silence. With that instinct that is only reasoning reaching a conclusion faster than the steps of logic can add up the facts, she realized Frank Hallet was standing somewhere in the rainy Saturday afternoon, breathing into a telephone. She fought to sound calm, and when she spoke, her voice was too flat, too level, too controlled.

"Mr. Hallet?"

Where was he? In the real estate office? At home? At a pay telephone somewhere? It did not matter; he knew where she was, and he was waiting.

"I know it's you, Mr. Hallet. This afternoon everyone else is at the football game." She put an edge on her voice, that same edge she had heard women in London use when talking to sales clerks and waitresses. "Mr. Hallet, you should know I've told my father about last Saturday night. I'm afraid he felt he had to report your behavior to the police. They're watching this house this very minute."

She should have hung up. She stayed on, she realized, an instant too long before she pressed the switch in the cradle. She wanted nothing in the way she ended the call to let the man know more of the terror she felt than he already knew.

In the hall she picked up Mario's wet clothes and carried them to the hearth. She dropped his muddy boots, spread his shirt across the back of the rocker, and hung the socks from the armrest. His Levis she shook out and draped between the coffee table and the hearth.

With the poker she prodded wadded newspaper into the embers till the paper burst into flame. She added chips of bark from the woodbox and laid on another log. From the phonograph records she drew one disc from its sleeve. She adjusted the sound to low, and Liszt's Piano Concerto began to fill the room.

A sock fell from the arm of the rocker. She picked it up and a finger found a hole gaping above the heel.

At footsteps on the stairs she turned.

It was a trick of the light, of course, but for a moment her father, complete to a pipe at his mouth, stood in silhouette.

"Nice robe," Mario said. "Even fits."

Rynn threw the sock onto the rocker and hurried to stand at the foot of the stairs in front of the boy who wrapped a towel around his neck. He drew the pipe from his mouth and handed it down to her.

"Found it in the pocket."

Rynn's hand closed around the pipe feeling its familiar shape. With her other hand she reached up to the boy.

"You'll be warm by the fire."

In the firelight she knelt behind him to dry his hair with the towel.

"Who called?"

"No one."

She toweled his hair.

"Rynn?"

"Really. Whoever it was didn't say a word."

"Hallet?"

"Of course."

"Creep," he said and coughed.

"You're still shivering."

From the couch she unfolded a blanket and wrapped it around him.

"Here. Closer to the fire. And, Mario? Don't shiver. Please?"

"Okay," he said, as if he had some power over the chill the hot bath, the wool robe, and the blanket had not warmed away.

"You're like ice."

Her hands went over his shoulders and down inside his robe to his chest. She rubbed.

"That feel better?"

Mario kissed her arm as it brushed his face. It was the first time his lips had touched her. The touch caused a silence that neither of them could think of any way to fill.

With the palms of her hands she stroked his breast, letting them stray to his thin ribs and to the firm young stomach muscles that jumped under her touch.

"Getting dark," he said, but most of the sound stuck in his throat.

She rested her head against the hollow between his neck and shoulder. Her hands smoothed their way to his back and up to his shoulders. When they started down again, over his chest, his ribs, onto his quivering belly, he stifled a gasp.

Her breath was hot against his ear. "Mario."

He said nothing.

"If you want," she said in a voice so quiet he might not have heard, "I'll get into bed with you."

Not daring to look at her, he cleared his throat.

"Or if you'd rather, we can stay by the fire. I'll move the couch."

She got up, pushing the coffee table to one side and turning the couch around to face the fire. She reached for the blanket to spread it over the cushions, but Mario clasped it around him.

He followed her bidding and sat on the couch, his head hanging down between hunched shoulders. He did not see her draw off her black sweater and unzip her Levis and push them down her smooth, golden legs. She climbed past him onto the couch, lay beside him, and pulled the blanket over them.

She snuggled close to him, her face against his neck. She could feel him tense as he waited for her whispered words.

"Better?"

He nodded but did not speak. His arm went around her and they lay wrapped together looking up at the ceiling where the firelight moved the shadows of the rafters. The concerto ended in a final rush, a burst of shimmering notes. The player clicked off.

The only sound now was the pattering rain.

Mario coughed, coughed again and covered his face with his hand. Rynn's fingers touched his mouth.

"Sshh."

They watched the shadows deepen on the ceiling as the only glow in the room burned low.

"Your hair," she said.

"What about it?"

"Dry?"

The question gave her the right to reach over and run her fingers through the boy's tangle of curls. Her hand lingered, stroking his head. The muscles in the back of his neck were rock hard.

"Mario the Magician?"

"I know what you're going to ask."

"Have you ever?"

"Hundreds of times."

"Like me and hashish," she said, turning and kissing his neck. Her finger trailed across his face.

But Mario did not laugh. She let her hand fall to his shoulder.

They stared up into the rafters and the ceiling, now almost totally in shadow.

Was it an hour later? Two hours? The fire cast no more glow. On the hearth the embers were dull. Rynn shivered. The one blanket was no longer enough to keep them warm. Raising herself on an elbow she turned to look at Mario. To her surprise she found his eyes glistened with tears.

She whispered, "I'll get another blanket."

He shook his head, and she wondered at his silence. For such a long time he had said nothing that she had begun to think perhaps he wanted her to leave him.

"Once you're warm, it'll be all right," she said. "It'll be lovely. Really it will. You'll see. . . ."

As she rose he turned his face from her, his shoulders were shaking. He was crying.

Rynn returned to the couch and lay perfectly still. The last time she had reached out to him, she had felt him pull away. What could she do?

"Mario?"

He was sitting up and reaching across her he pulled his still-damp shirt from the rocker and drew it across them.

"Mario?"

He said nothing. He drew on the shirt.

She found herself supplying the excuse. "They expect you home for dinner?"

Buttoning his shirt he nodded.

Never had words seemed so powerless.

"Mario?"

The boy slid his white legs from the couch.

She couldn't let him go.

Every instinct demanded she say something, something to make him stop buttoning his shirt . . .

"It wasn't your fault," she said and as soon as she said the words she felt him tense, and she wished very much she had said nothing. She should have said nothing and stifled her instincts. Up till now she had not questioned these impulses. Now they were failing her. What should she have said? For the last hour she had said nothing, or very nearly nothing, and that had not helped either.

Mario pulled on one leg of the trousers. He stood to draw on the other leg.

She dared speak again, only because she could not face the silence.

"Would it be so terrible if you didn't go? I mean if your family did find out about us?"

As if angry with his shirt he jammed it down over his hips and zipped up his trousers.

"Mario?"

He had worked on one damp sock and was searching for the other.

"Your Uncle Ron knows—"

"They'd want to know all about you. Every goddamn thing, I'm not as good at lying as you are."

"He didn't say that to hurt me," she whispered to herself.

He reached out for his wet shoes.

"Like your father said in that letter. Since when do they let kids do what they want?"

She rose. Her bare feet felt the hearthstones, and she wrapped the blanket around her. Without a word she followed him out of the parlor unable to think of a way to stop him from rolling his bicycle through the hall and opening the door.

Outside a soft rain fell, the drops sparkled in the shine of the spotlight. She handed him her father's macintosh, and Mario drew on the coat and turned the collar up to his ears against the rain.

"Come back after?"

Did he hear her?

She heard him cough. He was on his bicycle and gone into the night. Rynn shut the door and went back into the sitting room. Wrapping the blanket around her she sat alone in the dark.

15

LATER THAT EVENING the house was dark except for a faint red glow in the fireplace.

A tap at the front door went unanswered.

Nothing in the dark moved.

A louder tap, a knock. Then another.

Upstairs a light sprang on and in its glow Rynn appeared on the stairs tugging her sweater over her head and yanking it down to the top of her jeans. She hurried down to the hall. At the door she stopped.

"Who is it?"

"Ron Miglioriti."

Her hand on the lock, she paused to glance into the sitting room. The couch had been shoved from the fireplace and was back where it usually stood; all of Mario's clothes were gone; she had even taken the blanket upstairs. There was nothing about the room, nothing the officer should not see, no reason not to open the door.

Ron Miglioriti wore the same civilian clothes he had worn the previous Saturday. Only his shirt was different. At the collar and the cuffs, the shirt, undoubtedly new, frothed into lace.

"Hi," he said with his wide grin. "Looks like I'm making my usual Saturday night call."

Rynn stepped back from the door, a way of saying that it was all right—if the officer wanted to, he could come into her house; he was welcome.

"Are you all right?"

"Of course. I'm fine."

Miglioriti's grin split into one of his dazzling smiles.

"Just checking."

"I mean I appreciate it, but you really shouldn't worry about me so." She wondered if the policeman noticed that she had picked up the expression—*I mean*—from Mario. She doubted that. The man was too busy concentrating on trying to keep everything he said sounding unofficial, off-hand.

"I was coming by anyway."

"Cup of tea?"

"Can't stay."

"Your pumped-up lady waiting?" Rynn smiled. "Sorry. I guess I got that expression from Mario. Makes me sound rather a smartass, doesn't it?"

"That is one thing you'll never be."

What did he mean by that? Did the policeman mean there were other things she was? He probably did not mean that at all. Sometimes American English was so vague. You never knew what people really meant. She hated that.

He was looking into the parlor. Rynn switched on the light so the man could see that in there everything was in order.

"All alone?" he asked.

"My father's here."

Miglioriti did not look at her, but continued to study the room, making no reply.

She knew that he said nothing because to answer her would be to begin a chain of questions and answers about her father, none of which he could accept as the truth. He had done that twice. He was no longer going to play her game. Not a third time.

"Rynn, I think by now you realize I don't believe what you've been telling me about your father."

"No?" Her voice was more than cool, almost haughty.

"Look. I can understand why you might want to make it seem like your father was here if Mario was. I mean you don't have to tell me the way a small town talks. But what I can't figure out is why you insist on going on with this pretense when both of us know your father isn't here. Your father hasn't been here. . . ."

The girl's eyes looked straight into his, a look that stopped him. He ran his fingers through his hair.

"And don't act like I've just kicked Her Majesty the Queen or something. I didn't believe you the first time you told me. Look. I've been hoping you were going to help me. I've been waiting for you to tell me where he is."

She continued to stare at him without answering.

"Now you *are* going to help me, aren't you?"

"I wonder if you realize how patronizing you sound."

"I'm sorry if that's the way I sound, but you haven't given me a straight answer yet." He moved to the studio door. "If I try to open this door are you going to tell me he's in there working?"

"No. But he *was* working. He was translating. All after-noon."

"I see." Miglioriti could not mask his annoyance at having allowed her to slip so easily back into her game. With exaggerated patience, like someone who has told a story too many times, repeating the lines till he was sick of them, he said, "But he isn't now? That it? Never mind. I haven't got all night. Look. What you do is your business, but . . ."

"Have I broken any laws?"

"Not that I know of."

"Have I done something wrong?"

"Rynn, why won't you tell me about your father?"

"Aren't you keeping your lady friend waiting?"

"Let me worry about that."

She tossed her head with enough arrogance to send her long hair back from her face. One hand smoothed the hair against her shoulder.

"What is it you want to know?"

"I want to know where your father is."

"Now?"

"That's right."

"Now he's upstairs. Resting."

Miglioriti was no longer smiling. "Look. I've been in this house three times. Each time I've been impressed by how very good you are with words. The way you speak, you're very careful. If you ask me, a goddamn lot *too* careful."

"You don't believe he's upstairs?"

"I'm afraid I've never believed a single thing you've said."

The girl ran to the foot of the stairs.

"Father?" She ran halfway up the stairs and called again. "Father?"

Before Miglioriti could determine if he heard a voice answer her, Rynn ran down the stairs and crossed the hall to him.

"He'll be right down."

"Mr. Jacobs?" Miglioriti's voice sounded loud as a gunshot in the tiny house.

The girl spoke. "You're perfectly right of course. I haven't always been telling the truth. That's because"—she looked down at her black sweater and gave the waistband a tug —"well, you see, the truth is, my father's not always well." She stopped as if there were more, much more, she could not say.

The officer made it clear that he would wait, he would hear *all* of what she chose to say.

"You see, poets aren't like other people."

"A minute ago you accused *me* of sounding patronizing."

She didn't apologize. "Perhaps you simply don't realize. I mean Edgar Allen Poe was a drug addict. Dylan Thomas drank himself to death. Sylvia Plath took her own life."

"We're talking about your father."

"My father," she said, "sometimes goes into that room off the hall and locks the door. In there he keeps something in a drawer. It won't do any good to ask me what it is; I don't know. But when he locks the door I know it's because he doesn't want me to see him the way he becomes."

Miglioriti's face showed nothing, neither acceptance nor disbelief. The girl walked with him to the door. Miglioriti rattled the lock. The door did not open.

"If he's not in there now, why is the door locked?"

"You don't believe me when I say he's upstairs?"

"I want to go into that room."

"Can the police in America simply knock down doors? I mean don't you need a search warrant or something?"

He held out his hand.

"Please give me the key."

The girl ran to the foot of the stairs. "Father!"

Miglioriti repeated the words. "Give me the key!"

"It's upstairs." Too quickly, she added, "He has it."

"Then get it!"

Angrily, she turned, and climbed the stairs.

While she was gone Miglioriti inspected the living room. He lifted cushions from the couch, found nothing and tossed them back in place. He opened the woodbox and brought the lid down silently. He took the book of poems from the mantelpiece.

"You asked for the key."

He turned to find Rynn standing in the hall holding a shining bit of brass. Placing the book back on the mantelpiece, he went to her, took the key, crossed the hall to the door, and put it in the lock. He was turning the key when he heard the voice from the top of the stairs.

"Yes, Officer?"

An astonished Miglioriti turned to look up at the second floor. Silhouetted against the light at the top of the stairs was a man in a robe and what looked like gray flannel trousers. The man took a step or two down the stairs, then grasped for the railing.

"I hope you'll forgive me if I don't come all the way down. Bit under the weather, I'm afraid."

"Father, this is Officer Miglioriti, I've told you about."

"Good evening, sir," the officer managed to say. "I'm sorry to bother you."

"Quite all right. I'm the one to apologize. Apparently you've found me hard to find. You see, I have been intending to thank you for coming round, though I seriously doubt my daughter and I need worrying about. Rynn, don't simply stand there. Get our friend a drink."

"No thank you, sir." Miglioriti crossed to the bottom of the stairs. When the light caught the older man's face the officer could see Jacob's gray hair, poetically long, and his carefully trimmed beard.

"I confess to being a bit tired. Your New York City is not, I'm afraid, a particularly restful place. But that, as they say, is neither here nor there. Now, how can my daughter and I help you?"

"No problem, sir." As Miglioriti's fingers burrowed in his hair, he looked toward the door. Rynn could see that nothing the man might do or say could disguise how desperately he longed to leave this house.

"Rynn, nip into my study and get one of my books, will you?"

The girl pushed open the door Miglioriti had unlocked.

"And a pen," the poet called.

When she returned with a book and a pen the bearded man on the stairs was leaning against the wall. He was talking:

"I *do* apologize that up till now we've missed one another." He held out his hand to the girl. "Rynn tells me we've promised you an autographed copy." He coughed.

"If you'd be kind enough to spell Miglioriti."

"Ron will be okay."

"Of course."

Jacobs wrote in the book and handed it to Rynn who brought it to the policeman.

"Thank you, sir."

"My daughter tells me you have a young lady waiting out in your car. Would she care for a copy of my book?"

"She's not exactly the poetry type." Miglioriti laughed. The man on the stairs, just a moment behind in catching the joke, joined in the laughter.

Miglioriti was backing toward the door. "Good to meet you, sir."

The man on the stairs pulled the collar of his robe close to his neck and waved. "A pleasure meeting you, Officer. Unless I return to England on business soon, I expect that doubtlessly we'll be seeing one another," he added, with a chuckle, "socially, that is."

"Good night, sir."

"Good night." He had seemed very tired, but his farewell had a cheery English lilt as he turned and slowly mounted the stairs.

At the door Miglioriti turned to look at Rynn.

"Guess I owe you an apology."

"Why? For doing your duty?"

He handed the girl the key.

"Good night." He opened the front door and disappeared into the dark.

"Good night," Rynn called.

16

RYNN WATCHED the patrol car disappear down
the lane, then slowly shut the door, locked it, and, with a
burst of wild laughter, dashed up the stairs taking them
three at a time.

"Mario the Magician!"

Jubilant, she raced to her bedroom, then, at the doorway,
stopped herself, consciously determining, striving, to make
her joy last. She leaned against the door's wooden frame.
Her bedroom was white and yellow. The tongue-in-groove
paneling, the slanting ceiling under the eaves—all gleamed
white. Bright yellow curtains dotted with tiny white roses
reflected the yellow lamplight, cheerful as May sunshine. A
bedspread the same color was thrown back and spilled to
the floor leaving the bed a blaze of yellow and white.

Her room. Always her room alone. But now Mario, in her
father's robe, sat on the edge of the bed, a box of yellow
Kleenex in his lap.

"Your voice," she said. "Absolutely perfect. So deep."

"That's this damn cold." He smothered a sneeze with a
tissue.

"I mean you really sounded English."

"You write good dialogue." He turned his bearded pro-
file to the girl, thrust the pipe into his mouth, and spoke as
he had to Miglioriti. "Rynn tells me we've promised you a
copy of my book."

"Absolutely super!" she giggled, her face shining with
happiness.

"How do you spell Miglioriti?"

"That was your idea!" They both broke into laughter. In
her glee, Rynn almost stumbled as she made her way to the
bed.

"What's so bloody marvelous is it's all so airtight. Your
Uncle Ron won't, but even if he takes the book to the bank
or to the Hallet's real estate office and compares the signature on the check form or the lease with the one in the book,
it's one father already signed."

Mario sniffed into a Kleenex.

"So you see, you're not only a bloody good actor, you're
a marvelous forger as well."

Slowly and carefully, as if lifting a scab from a healing
wound, Mario pulled off the moustache and whiskers.

"Talent, that's me," he said lifting a moustache hair from
his lip.

Rynn drew her black sweater over her head, struggled
out of her jeans and jumped onto the bed, grabbed the
beard from the boy and hung it on a bed post. Looking up
at it, they suddenly roared with laughter.

When she was calm enough to speak, she said,

"If you hadn't come back, how would I ever have known
your Uncle Ron was coming here tonight?"

"I would have had to—as you say—'ring up.'"

"You mustn't. Ever. We've already decided that." She
untied the belt of his robe and spread the collar from his
shoulders.

"I would have come back anyway."

"I hoped you would."

"Except . . ."

"My darling, I *know*."

"I mean after what happened—or didn't happen the first time—you don't know how that makes a guy feel. Jesus, I mean I was really scared it might be the same all over again."

Rynn kissed his white shoulder.

"Wow," he said. "I mean I should have told my Uncle Ron what he was interrupting, right?"

Because the girl's face was on his back, her voice was muffled.

"A gentleman," she said with an exaggerated English voice, "does not tell. *Ever*."

"Maybe in England guys don't. Here guys never shut up about it."

She withdrew her face from his shoulder and watched as Mario pulled off the robe and dropped back on the pillow, a huge grin spreading across his face.

"I'll bet half—hell, most of the guys on the football team are still only talking about it." His eyes met Rynn's. The light that filtered through the yellow lampshade made her eyes greener than he had ever seen them. He reached out and began counting her freckles with his forefinger.

"You know I won't tell."

She poked his bare chest and her finger drew two lines.

"There. You just crossed your heart."

"I mean it, Rynn."

She smiled, but even as she did she felt hot tears spring into her eyes.

He said, "How can you even start to think I don't trust you?" She had never seen his black eyes so solemn. "I mean most people don't go through as much as we have—not even in a whole, entire lifetime."

Lightly, Rynn kissed Mario behind the ear.

"No one will know about us."

She moved, but only to draw the sheet and blanket up over their shoulders. She settled her chin on Mario's chest so she could look up into his face.

"See how I need you?"

"Unless," he said, his voice an English accent again, "unless I return to England on business, doubtless we'll be seeing one another."

At his words they pressed closer to each other.

"The thing is"—the girl's voice was far away—one of those voices that hesitates to put the fear the speaker feels into words—"they're bound to wonder about where you are."

"Who's they?"

"You asked that before."

"You didn't answer."

"Everyone. Your family for a start. Your uncle." She could barely bring herself to add, "Hallet."

Mario knew she had more to say.

"They already wonder why they hardly ever see me in the village." She was smiling to herself. "We can't have them wondering about you."

"What are you smiling about?"

"You. Me."

"No. You were thinking about something else."

"Emily Dickinson."

"And how she never left her house unless she had to?"

"'Unless emergency leads me by the hand.'"

"You think she had some stud hidden away up in her bedroom?"

"I hope so." She giggled, her soft lips on his.

"Still," she whispered, "we have to be careful."

"Right."

"Think ahead. Think ahead and be ready for them all the time."

"Rynn?"

"Mm?"

"You think we can?"

"Of course."

"Live your way, I mean. Remember when I asked you if it would be so awful if you *did* have to play their game?"

She lifted her lips from his face. Now it was her eyes that challenged him.

"If we played their game you'd be home right now eating your Mom's terrible spaghetti and watching horrible TV. I'd be all alone."

Mario turned away and seemed to study the slant of the eaves.

"Mario?"

"Mm?"

"You do see, don't you?"

"Sure."

"I mean that's why you did everything you did. If we don't go on we'll be like the rest of them. You ever look at them? I mean really look? You don't want to be like the rest of them, do you?"

"I guess not."

She raised herself on her elbow to stare down at the boy.

He did not look at her when he said very quietly, "You ever think maybe I'm playing your game?"

"You did it because you want to!"

"I did it because I love you."

She searched his face.

"You know what?"

"What?"

"You're trying not to sneeze." She reached across him to the night table to pull up a handful of yellow tissues.

The boy grabbed the tissue before he exploded.

"You're going to catch my cold," he said.

"I wouldn't be without it." To prove how wholeheartedly she welcomed the idea, she kissed his mouth fiercely. It was true; his face, his forehead were burning.

"You're really hot."

"Wonder why?"

They both giggled.

"Mario?"

"Mm?" The very English *mm* was something he had learned from Rynn.

"When I told you I don't mind being alone, I lied."

More gently than she had done, Mario kissed Rynn's face, and eyes, a place, until this minute, Rynn had never imagined could be kissed. She knew he was tasting the hot tears that squeezed through her closed lashes and ran down over her cheeks. Crying, laughing—all her feelings were changing so quickly she had no way, no time to think why, only time to feel—so much was happening.

"I do try to be brave, the way my father asked me to be, but sometimes everything frightens me so—"

"Sshh." The boy's lips sealed hers.

"Dear, dear Mario, don't ever go—Promise?"

From head to foot Mario's hard young body fitted hers. As changeable as her laughter and tears, he was on fire one second, the next second, shaking with cold.

Giving and taking comfort in everything they could give and take, every part of them sought to make themselves one till it was impossible for either to know the comforter from the one being comforted.

17

"THE SMELL of burning leaves in the air makes me think of London," Rynn was talking to Officer Miglioriti on Tuesday afternoon when the sun was bright, but the day was biting cold enough that she wore her duffle coat. "Isn't it incredible. All these leaves—all the leaves in the world, actually, have to go so we can have a whole new world full of leaves next year."

Officer Miglioriti had not come to talk about autumn leaves, and though he was trying to make his presence seem unplanned, he was growing impatient.

Rynn had been cutting back the chrysanthemums, breaking off the dead zinnia stalks, raking the leaves into a heap where they smoldered red, and white smoke curled up.

Through the smoke she had seen the patrol car coming down the lane. Before the driver could see her screened by the underbrush, she had hurried into the house and lit a Gauloise to fill the parlor with the pungent smell of tobacco. Outside the window, beyond the drifting wood smoke, she watched the policeman stop his car. When she was satisfied the room was filled with the smell of the French cigarette she had hurried outside to throw the Gauloise into the fire before Miglioriti strode up the walk.

"Nice day," the officer had said.

"Lovely."

"The English," the girl said, "are mad about gardens."

They talked casually as she waited for Miglioriti to tell her why he had come. She rolled green acorns and brown horse chestnuts into the fire. At last the policeman spoke:

"While the ground's still damp, it might be a good time to have a look and see if you and your father have had any visitors."

"All right," she said.

"I don't want to bother you."

"No bother. I'd love to look with you. I mean if you don't mind. I adore detective stories. You ever read Agatha Christie? Most of her murders take place in England, in the most super old country places—not that places like that actually exist, but they're lovely to think about all the same. . . ."

They walked side by side to the corner of the house.

"In England we always had a garden. Even in London, a charming little patch in the back all in dahlias"—she pronounced them *daylias*—"and snapdragons, gladioli, and delphiniums. Or is it 'delphiniae'?"

They were approaching the grape arbor.

"What are we looking for?" she asked with too much enthusiasm, as if she were joining in the detective charade. "Footprints?"

With his foot Miglioriti scraped leaves away from the soil. She saw at once that he could not overlook that the earth here had been freshly turned.

Much as the officer had, she managed to sound very offhand when she explained this was a new tulip bed that her father and she had worked up. They had it in parrot tulips.

The officer studied the soil and the leaves that lay on it.

"You know parrot tulips?" She went chattering on, a typical English gardener showing a visitor the grounds. "All ragged edges, terribly brilliant colors actually. That's why they call them parrot tulips I expect."

She hurried through the crackling dry grass to lean inside the open window under the grape arbor.

"Father, it's Officer Miglioriti."

She turned to the officer. "Do you want to come in?"

Miglioriti glanced around; he picked a cluster of shriveled grapes and tossed them away.

"It was you I came to see."

"That's very flattering." She was bubbling with cheerfulness.

Miglioriti lifted an apple that still hung from the crucified tree pinned against the house.

"Take it if you like," she said.

But the officer let the apple drop back against the wall.

"I came to see you."

"So you said."

"I better tell you I don't understand you at all." His black eyes searched her face until Rynn, sensing she must make some move, worked her white hands to tug her black sweater down over her hips.

"I mean what don't you understand?"

The man's heavy police shoes scraped leaves across the earth.

"Take a look," he said.

"Footprints?"

"See for yourself."

"They tell you anything?"

"Inconclusive," he said without investing the word with any meaning, a most usable word in his work, a word that explained nothing but ended matters.

His back was turned, and Rynn could not see his face, but she felt he was about to repeat that he did not understand her. She would have to be alert.

He spoke. "You haven't asked about Mario."

A sob broke from her. Her eyes stung with tears. He had broken her guard which was exactly what he wanted.

"Since Saturday: Three whole days I haven't heard . . ."

"You didn't know?"

"Know what?"

"He's in the hospital."

She shut her eyes and waited.

"Pneumonia."

"I didn't even know. How serious?"

"Without antibiotics he probably would have died."

"Nobody told me!"

"I'm sorry. I thought you knew."

"How would I know? You should have told me right away!"

The girl no longer fought to control herself. In her tears she had forgotten what lay beneath the earth on which they were standing.

"Out here in your lane you keep very much to yourself."

"I have to see him!"

"Can you go now?"

Rynn was already running for the lane and the police car. Miglioriti walked back to the smoldering pile of leaves and scattered the fire.

She was waiting at the car. "You've seen him?"

The officer nodded.

"How was he?"

"Delirious. Mumbling. Talking out loud."

Rynn felt herself go cold and empty. Her heart slammed in her throat.

"Talking wild."

"Yes?"

"About the two of you."

"Yes?"

"Saying how much he loves you."

Rynn's face was wet and shining with tears. She fumbled in her pockets. She drew out a comb, ran it through her hair, dropped it. Her hands went back to her pockets.

"I need my wallet. I—" She turned and ran into the house.

When she came down the stairs she found Miglioriti in the sitting room folding the cardboard lid back on the jelly glasses.

She waited in the hall.

"I'm ready."

But the policeman took another moment with the carton.

"She never did come by?"

"Who?"

"Mrs. Hallet."

"No."

"She told her son she was coming by."

"Never did. Can we go to the hospital now?"

"She won't be needing them." He added quickly, "That's only my opinion, you understand?"

Rynn kept her voice steady, but inside her pockets she felt cold sweat on her hands.

"You've . . . found her?"

"Not yet."

"But, you said . . ."

He tapped the carton with his foot. The glasses clinked. He strode past the gateleg table, across the braided rug.

"Again—and it's only my opinion—which, if you repeat, I'll have to deny—but I don't think we ever will find her."

"No?" She ached to ask the officer *why*, what reason he had, that made him believe that no one would ever find the woman.

"I saw Hallet this morning. He was driving her Bentley."

In her most matter-of-fact voice Rynn asked, "Why shouldn't he?"

"Come on. We can talk about it in the car. Ready?"

Rynn ran to the study door and knocked.

"Father, I'm going to the hospital with Officer Miglioriti. To see Mario. I'll call from there and let you know when I'll be home. Bye." Rynn locked the front door, switched on the spotlight, and raced through the smoke to the lane.

In the police car the radio crackled: A woman at the Safeway had locked herself out of her car.

"What do you say we let her frozen food melt," said Miglioriti, "while I get you to the hospital first?"

Rynn had never been in a police car before. She sat in silence waiting for the radio to crackle back to life.

"About Mario," Miglioriti said, "you can relax. He's getting everything he needs."

"That's easy for you to say."

The officer did not look at her, but he smiled. "I hope that under the same circumstances that big blonde of mine would talk that way."

The car turned from the lane onto the road that led to the highway.

"Back at your house we were talking about Frank Hallet driving his mother's car. You asked how he got the keys."

"No," said the girl. "What I asked was, why shouldn't he?"

Rynn prayed the radio would come to life, interrupt with something more than a stranded woman in a supermarket parking lot, something that would demand Miglioriti's full attention.

"Mario didn't tell you Mrs. Hallet wouldn't let her own son drive her car?"

"I guess he may have."

"You didn't know that since she's been gone the car's been locked?"

Rynn realized each question could be the one to trap her. And now that the questions were coming faster than she could think, her only defense was to make no reply.

"Or that we had to tow it from in front of her office to Mario's dad's garage?" Miglioriti slowed for a car backing out of a driveway.

The thought of Mario lying in the hospital never left her. She was sick with worry, unable to think about what the man was saying, yet she knew she must stay alert for the policeman. Right now, was he questioning her or simply talking out his thoughts?

The officer waited for the girl to ask how Hallet had managed to open the car and when she did not, he supplied the question.

"How do you suppose he got in?"

"Called a locksmith?"

"Yeah." Miglioriti seemed disappointed that the girl's logic had so thoroughly dispelled his mystery.

"I mean, isn't that what you'd do?" she asked. "I know I would."

"If I never expected to see my mother again."

"Have you asked him?"

"With the Hallets you don't ask. You *talk*, but you talk very politely and even then you don't press. Frank Hallet is a rich man now. We'll be seeing a lot of Hallet—driving around in that Bentley."

"You don't like him, do you?"

"Let's just say I hope all of you see the day that son of a bitch makes the wrong move. Till that day you'll have to watch him—driving around in her car."

He stopped at a light. He reached out and buttoned the top of Rynn's coat. "No. I don't like him."

They drove on in silence.

"What do you want to bet he even shows up at the police raffle tonight?"

Miglioriti turned the car onto the highway, but in the direction that led away from the village. He must have felt her confusion.

"Mario's not in the village. The doctor wanted him in the hospital in town."

That made Mario's condition sound even worse.

"You got money for the bus, so you can get home?"

Rynn nodded.

The car windows began to cloud till the officer turned on the windshield defroster. In the streets the traffic grew heavy. Miglioriti lowered his head to see the light at an intersection change from red to green.

"There's the hospital on the right." He pulled the car to the curb.

Rynn wiped the mist from the side window to look at the giant gray building. Somewhere in there lay Mario. Her hand went to the door handle.

"Before you go, I've got something I have to tell you." She scanned the huge building.

"Did you notice when I said what I did about Hallet that I said I hoped all of you would see the day when he makes his wrong move and gets caught up with? I said that because I won't be here. You won't be seeing me any more."

It was a moment before Rynn, deep in worry over Mario, realized what the man was saying.

"I'm going out to California."

"But you work here!"

"Not any more." He pulled his cap off. "I finally did it. I quit."

A cold lump of fear strangled any attempt to speak, but

she managed to gasp, "Can you? I mean quit—just like that."

"Not just like that. I've been thinking about it for over a year." He put his cap on the seat between them and his hand ran around the black edge of the steering wheel. "It means I'll lose my seniority here. I'll have to start over in San Francisco, but I figure that in the long run it's the right move."

"No!"

"I've made up my mind."

"Is it because of that girl?"

"She likes the idea of living out there, too—"

"But you just said you'd lose your seniority."

"The truth is I don't see all that much future for me here. Not in this town."

Rynn watched the patch she had cleared on her window streak with fog.

"Without getting technical about it, there's a board that reviews all officers up for advancement."

"And Hallet's on that board?"

"No. But I don't want to wait and find out he has friends who are—"

"You can't go!"

"I'll miss you, Rynn."

She sat in the stifling heat feeling sweat covering her brow.

"One of my biggest worries was about leaving you. Does that come as a surprise?"

Rynn, incapable of answering, shook her head.

"I never liked the idea of you being out there in the lane with Hallet hanging around—not when I thought you were all alone." His other hand met the first circling the steering wheel. "I'll have to confess that up till I met your father I figured that's what you were—all alone. See, what I really couldn't figure out was *why*—every time I came out there—

you put on this big act about him being at home. Part of that cleared up the night I found out about you and Mario. You wanted to cover for him. Okay. I mean you two are pretty young, but I guess what you do is strictly your own business. Still, it wasn't till I finally met your father that I could relax about Hallet. Coming out there today was just sort of a last check to see if Hallet had got the word. Now, I mean since you're not alone, I can go and know that you're safe."

Rynn wanted nothing more than to cry out her need for help. She squeezed back hot tears.

"Knowing you're all right means a lot to me, Rynn."

They sat in silence.

"I'll be in to say good-bye to Mario before I go, but I probably won't get another chance to see you. . . ."

The girl waited.

"So I guess this is good-bye. . . ."

She pressed her face to his cheek. The slam of the door covered her sob.

18

"I DON'T GO from my home, unless emergency leads me by the hand," Emily Dickinson had said.

Rynn knew the risk she ran by going to see Mario. This town, this hospital, this was the world. She was no longer able to hide in her little house behind the trees in the lane where she could close and lock the door. How could she know who she might meet in there? How could she be ready for the questions they might ask?

They. Mario had once asked who *they* were. That was the danger the two of them lived with. *They* could be anyone.

The first person she met, the nurse behind the reception desk, stiff with starch, was one of those large, loud-voiced women Rynn found so fast to laugh, so quick to help, that she was beginning to think it was women like these who kept America running. These women were everywhere, capable, friendly, and terribly overwhelming.

"He's up one flight and down the hall. Four-oh-seven. Just listen. You can't miss him. It's the room that sounds like an Italian wedding." She pronounced the word *Eyetalian*.

"Has he got visitors?" she asked.

The nurse, who reminded Rynn of a blonde American movie star she had seen once but whose name she did not know, glanced down at a massive arm and a tiny gold watch.

"This time on a Tuesday afternoon? I doubt it. You can go on up. Oh, wait just a minute."

The girl held her breath. Had something gone wrong already?

The blonde woman went into an office and returned to thrust a pot of yellow chrysanthemums at her.

Rynn was not sure what she was expected to do.

"Take them. He might as well enjoy them."

The nurse found the girl's green eyes wide over the yellow flowers.

"They came for somebody else, but she's not here any more. . . ."

"Thank you," said Rynn.

The woman grinned. "He's a real cutie, right? If I were you, I'd get up there before his whole family shows up and starts yelling."

Outside Room 407 Rynn heard nothing, even when she leaned close to the panel to listen. She had decided, if any guests were calling on Mario, she would come back later. Because she heard nothing, she opened the door. Inside, an accordion-fold plastic divider was pushed halfway back. In the bed near the door a fat man looking like an unpleasant Buddha peered through slit eyes at a movie on television. No sound came from the set. A girl of perhaps twelve, who looked as if she had eaten too many spaghetti dinners, squatted on the floor munching chocolates from an enormous gold-foil box, scattering the empty little brown paper cups around her like autumn leaves.

A boy of Rynn's age, a sturdier version of Mario, sat near the other bed. He did not look up from the full-color pages of a comic book.

Then she saw Mario, very small, almost lost in the bed across the room. His face was not white like the sheets, but a horrible fish-gray that made Rynn gasp. She was sure he could not look more gray if he were dead.

Holding the flowers, Rynn stared in dismay, only vaguely aware that the girl who had been munching chocolates had looked up and whispered something. She tried to sort out her panic. Mario had been ill, terribly ill, she knew that. He was still in the hospital, but she never imagined Mario, her Mario, Mario the Magician, could look like this. . . .

The girl on the floor seemed compelled to explain what she was doing.

"Mr. Pierce in the other bed's deaf so he doesn't mind if the sound's not on." Her voice was low. "And my mother says when we're with Mario we have to be quiet. Not that we'd keep him awake." She pushed the shiny gold box of chocolates at the girl.

"Have one. Some dumb-dumb sent them to Mario."

Rynn made a sign; she wished none of the candy.

"I'm Terry, his sister. The one over there improving his mind on comic books is Tom. He's the one who's really sick."

The boy glanced up from the adventures of Spider Man.

Terry poked among the chocolates, tested one by nibbling at the corner, frowned her disapproval at its caramel contents, and dropped it back in the box.

Would the hospital allow visitors, even his own brother and sister, if Mario were as ill as he looked?

"Pretty flowers," the girl said of the chrysanthemums. "You been here before?"

Rynn managed to move her head, meaning she had not been in this room, she had not seen Mario like this.

"He's okay now," said the girl digging a nutmeat from her teeth with the nail of her little finger.

Rynn spoke her first words. "Is that what the doctors say?"

"Sleepy though." Terry rummaged among the brown paper cups.

"You know him from school?"

Even the jolt of seeing Mario so drained of life was no excuse for half-considered answers. Rynn told herself she must weigh words. She was considering how to answer when the comic book spoke. "How can he know her at school?"

Rynn dared turn to the boy before her eyes dragged back to Mario. How much did this boy already know?

"I mean," Tom said to his sister, "he's a lot older." His next question was for Rynn. "Like how old are you?"

"Thirteen," Rynn said.

"Yeah?" The boy rolled the comic book into a tube. "I'm thirteen, too. How come I never see you at school?"

"Perhaps we don't go to the same school."

"I don't go to parochial school, do you?"

"No," said Rynn.

"Then how come?"

She looked at Mario and felt her heart would crack. She wanted nothing more than to burst into tears. The questions kept coming, much too fast, and she hoped to show, by staring intently at the boy in bed, that her mind was on Mario, not on questions about age and school.

"What school do you go to?" demanded the boy.

"Private school I'll bet," said the fat girl. "They teach them to talk that way."

"Around here?" Tom asked.

Rynn shut her eyes in an effort to block out the lifeless mask that was Mario. She had to think. She told herself these two were not being suspicious, this was the direct way of children. Children were *like* this. She reminded herself she knew few children. No. That was not true. She knew none if one didn't include Mario. He was no child. He was a person, not one of these chocolate-chewing, comic-book-reading creatures, so demanding. Were English children like this?—so terribly outspoken with everyone? She heard the boy speaking, again demanding.

"I asked you"—his voice was an accusation—"around here?"

"No. Not around here."

"You English or something?" asked Terry, dropping another rejected chocolate into the box.

"Yes."

"So where do you know Mario from?" Tom spoke in that flat American way that was neither friendly nor hostile, simply matter-of-fact.

"From his magic shows actually." Putting the yellow chrysanthemums on a bureau she suddenly wanted to scream at these two to get out so she could be alone with her Mario. "Parties," she found herself saying. "The Saturday before last he did a lovely show."

"Lovely," mimicked Terry, prissing her mouth into tea-party manners.

"He's a real hambone." Tom unrolled the comic book and returned to Spider Man.

"You know why he loves doing magic so much?" Terry said without allowing Rynn to answer. "It's his way of compensating. For being crippled."

"Bullshit," said the voice behind the comic book.

"Psychologically valid. You can ask anyone."

Rynn fought a wild urge to rush forward, to hold Mario against her. Instead, she found herself asking, "The doctors do say he's going to be all right?"

The voice behind the comic book said, "What do they know?"

"Right now he's full of antibiotics," said the girl.

"Drugs," said the boy.

Rynn felt if these two would get out of this room, if she could be alone with Mario, she could warm that deathly gray away from his warm, olive skin.

Wistfully, Terry abandoned the gold-foil box to a table. "I guess you must be thinking that my brother's not too many laughs to visit, being practically asleep and all."

Rynn found herself shrugging her shoulders, hands in pockets, helpless, fighting tears.

Beyond the window in the dusk, street lights were blinking on. A car horn blared.

"We're only waiting here for our Mom," Terry said. "She's late."

Rynn felt a chill. Mario's mother. Here? There would be more questions. They might even offer her a ride home. . . . She fought a growing sense of panic.

Tom closed his comic book and yawned. "You can go up close to him. He isn't contagious or anything. He's just full of so many drugs, he'll probably get hooked before he ever gets out of here." Laughing at his own black joke Tom left his chair.

"Go ahead. If you can, wake him up. Probably be good for him." He rattled against the plastic room divider. "You want me to close this thing?"

Rynn looked at him through tears. His smile reminded her of Mario's. He was drawing the plastic folds, making the room private around her as she stood motionless at the foot of the bed.

Once alone, Rynn rushed to the pillow.

"Mario?"

When the mask made no sign, Rynn wept, giving in at last to the utter helplessness she had felt from the moment she had seen his face.

"I love you." She said the words to herself.

Love had never been part of the plan she and her father had talked out in such detail.

Love. In this cold November twilight, without Mario she could not go on alone. She could not do what she had to do. If he had never been with her perhaps then she could, but not now . . .

Now, the most important thing in the world was for Mario to come out from behind the gray mask.

"*Survive,*" her father had said. But how could she help him?

If she was to survive, what she must do, she told herself, is to stop, stop and try to think. So far Mario's brother and sister believed she was only a friend. At any moment a woman would pull back the room divider. Mario's mother would be here in this room. She would ask all the questions which must never be answered.

Rynn kissed the boy. "I love you," she whispered.

Then she pushed out past the rattling plastic divider and ran.

19

LIGHTS OF THE CITY sparkled in the cold evening. Though she had no idea where she was going, Rynn knew she could not face returning to the cold, dark house where Mario's gray face would be staring at her in every room. Not yet. She rushed to lose herself in the city's hurrying crowds and warm bright lights.

In a coffee shop indistinguishable from the many glaringly new glass and plastic cafes she and her father had seen dotting American highways and streets, she climbed onto a vinyl counter stool and tried to study a menu imbedded in shining plastic from which a dozen kinds of hamburgers jumped out at her in full color. A waitress not many years older than Rynn, wearing a pumpkin-orange uniform pinned with a plastic lace handkerchief and plastic name tag, took her order and in a startlingly short time very red cream of tomato soup and four white crackers in a painfully tight cellophane pack slid across the counter.

A cheeseburger with a slice of pickle, a scrap of lettuce and a quartered tomato followed immediately.

Rynn shut her eyes against her tears. Mario's gray face filled her world.

Around her in the glaring fluorescent light voices were loud. The place was full of young mothers and fathers feeding noisy, clambering children hamburgers and French fries splotched with heaps of blood-red ketchup.

Rynn choked down a few spoonfuls of soup, one cracker, and the slice of pickle.

In spite of her trancelike state, she managed to pay the bill and leave, and she found herself walking. The lights were bright, but not warm, and soon she was bitterly cold and shivering, even with her hands deep in her pockets. She walked without plan, drifting, trancelike. Some of the shops were open, flashing with lights and glittering with the first decorations of Christmas, and it was only when she stood in front of a bookshop that she realized this is what she had been looking for. The shop door was locked.

Reflected in the dark display windows Rynn saw not the familiar image in duffle coat and Levis, but Mario's silent gray face staring at her, and she turned away.

Further along the street a movie theater's marquee flared white. Rynn, who had never been to a film alone, made another unplanned move and drew two dollars from her wallet to approach the box office.

The young woman behind the glass shook her head. The girl was not allowed to enter. Could not a girl of thirteen go to the cinema?

The woman behind the glass tapped on her window to draw Rynn's attention to a card. The movie was rated in such a way that children were forbidden entrance, even children, it seemed, with parents.

At another theater, just as full of light, the name Walt Disney encouraged Rynn to try again. Although she was not fond of the kind of fantasy the name meant to her, she believed she would be allowed to pay her money and enter.

At the box office a gaunt man with rimless eyeglasses

that glinted in the light demanded a student card, raising in Rynn a lump of fear that only melted as he explained that such a card would entitle her to a discount on tickets. She bought a card and a ticket and soon found herself in the warm dark that smelled of buttered popcorn. She sank down in the hot blackness and let brilliant colors and music surge over her.

But the color and the music could not wash away Mario's gray face.

As in the coffee shop she felt numb to her surroundings. The ever-changing pictures and sounds on the screen sped by, no more than a patchwork, a meaningless jumble. The picture ended and dim light revealed perhaps fifty people who waited while recorded music that sounded like Mantovani played. A few noisy children pounded up and down the carpeted aisles spilling soft drinks from waxed cups and scattering popcorn from cardboard boxes.

Another picture, a dog and a lot of guns blasting and children screaming, filled the screen.

Thinking of Mario, she wept.

Lights sprang on, startling Rynn into drying her wet eyes as a couple of dozen people wandered up the aisles pulling on heavy coats, trying not to drop their scarves and mittens.

At first as she stood at the bus stop, the night's cold did not bite too sharply. But by the time the marquee lights went off, and the street was black, and the last of the audience had left her alone to wait for the bus, a razor-wind was cutting through her duffle coat and Levis, forcing her to huddle against a fiercely bitter cold.

She was peering into the deserted street wondering if the bus would ever come when a car with a throbbing motor slowed and edged close to her. She backed away from the curb as the car windows rolled down and boys of high-school age, their faces dead white and splotched with pimples under the street light, whistled and called at her. One held out a cigarette.

Another made an indescribably evil sucking sound.

"You missed the last bus. Come on. Get in. We'll keep you warm!" Guffaws broke from the car.

Turning her back on the car Rynn faced the dark windows of a camera store where cold blank eyes of lenses stared at her. In the window's reflection she saw the car was not moving away, and her heart stopped as a back door opened and a boy in a leather jacket and jeans studded with shining metal emerged, motioning to the others.

The boy slid his fingers through his long hair and ambled across the sidewalk.

Rynn peered up and down the street. Out there in the night nothing moved.

Another youth uncoiled from the car making the kissing, sucking sound as he crossed the sidewalk to block her way ahead.

In a panic Rynn saw the windows reflect them as they closed in on her from both sides. Too late to run. She shrank into the doorway.

Now both youths were making the kissing, sucking sound, when a voice yelled from the car. Suddenly they stopped, turned and fled to the machine, which roared off.

At the curb a black and white police car slowed to stop.

One of two officers in the front seat tapped on his window and motioned for Rynn to come to the car.

When the window went down, Rynn saw the bottom half of the man's heavy face working up and down as he chewed gum.

"You live here in town?" His voice was surprisingly gentle.

She shook her head. "No," she added, hoping the one word would be enough of an answer.

Rynn told herself that she must think carefully, she must make no mistakes.

"Actually, I'm visiting from England," she said.

"They let little girls wander around at night like this in England?" The policeman's eyes looked up into the girl's and his jaw moved steadily.

"No. You see what happened was, I was with my cousin—at the cinema—Walt Disney actually—but she ran into this boyfriend of hers, and I, well I didn't want to tag along, you know?"

The cop reached and opened the back door.

"Before you freeze to death, get in. We'll take you home."

She moved to the door.

"That's awfully good of you. Thank you very much indeed. . . ." She was halfway into the car when she drew back and looked at the officer. "This might sound strange, but I don't have the address and I'm not at all sure I can tell how to get there. We always drive. Or take the bus." She smiled helplessly, and she added a shrug. "I guess all I really know is where to get off the bus."

The officer looked at her. His expressionless face gave her no feeling that he either believed or disbelieved her.

"I imagine," she said, "that really does sound most awfully stupid. . . ."

"How far you live from the bus stop?"

"Just one short street."

The man never stopped chewing. He turned to the other officer, a pale young man with close-cropped hair and a large Adam's apple.

"What time does the next bus come by?"

"Two, three minutes."

He turned back to Rynn. "Get in anyway. You can wait with us till it comes."

For three minutes, until the officers signaled the bus to

stop behind them, Rynn chattered gaily to the policemen, accepting a stick of Doublemint gum, telling them how much she was enjoying her visit to the States during her school holidays.

When she dropped her coins into the fare box, the bus driver, a black man with an Afro and a scrawny moustache, eyed her from behind dark glasses and said, in a deliberately casual tone, "Pretty late isn't it?"

Without answering, Rynn moved as far from him as possible to sit in the long seat at the back of the empty bus. And even though she could not actually see the man's eyes behind the sunglasses in the rearview mirror, she was certain he was watching her. Her imagination? She could no longer neglect any instinct, any feeling, any perception.

"Pretty late isn't it?" His soft voice echoed in her mind in much the same way as her language records. "Pretty late, isn't it?" Of course it was pretty late. It was terribly late, and if she could have thought of any way to avoid going back to the house in the lane tonight, if she could put off hurrying up the dark lane full of blowing leaves and running alone into that black house she would not be alone on this bus, sitting here with cold hands, weak legs, haunted by an awful emptiness.

Rynn pulled her duffle coat close, but she shivered in the molded plastic seat under the harsh, bright lights as the bus roared through the night.

Everything frightened her now.

The driver's black glasses peered into the rearview mirror. He *was* looking at her.

"Where do you want off?"

"Two more stops," she said.

She rose and moved slowly forward, timing her steps with the speeding bus, timing her arrival at the front door with the appearance of the landmark—the house with the iron deer on the lawn.

"Pretty late," the driver said slowing his hurtling bus till the wheels ground across roadside gravel.

"Yeah, pretty late," he said again.

Now that Rynn was about to leave, now that she knew the conversation could not last, she was suddenly bold. "What's that supposed to mean?"

"Means, little lady," he spoke in his own private kind of rhythm, "that it's pretty late."

The front door exploded open with a hiss.

"Little lady?"

"Mm."

"You got far to go?"

"I'll be all right."

"If you say so. Night, night."

The door smacked shut behind her and the tires spun off over the loose gravel. The bus rumbled away, two red lights in the distance growing smaller.

Rynn pulled her coat up around her ears and with her hands deep in her pockets, ran down the street toward the ocean. The drifts of leaves underfoot gave her feet an extra spring and she ran without stopping to gasp for breath for more than a block, though the cold air was giving her a headache. She reached the lane. The giant trunks of the elms stood black, pillars in a gothic cathedral, their swaying bare branches touching overhead like the ribs of a vault open to the clear night sky.

The first time she had seen the lane it had been full of summer light, checkered shade, flowers blazing in the gardens, insects buzzing, a dog barking.

Leaves flew past her in the dark.

Overhead the branches rattled together.

The night, a living presence, was in constant motion, shifting itself, sighing, breathing. She wondered if perhaps it, too, was trying to get warm.

She drove herself to run past the house of her nearest neighbor, the people who had gone to Florida for the winter. Their house stood black, the windowpanes glinting cold as ice in the night.

The lane had never held terror for her before.

If she ran, she told herself, she would be home in a few minutes. She almost came to a stop. She brushed a leaf from her face. It was true, she was almost home, and the thought filled her with trembling. Putting the key in the lock, pushing the door open into the hall, walking into the sitting room that no fire warmed, the room would seem even colder than the outdoors. There was nothing, nobody waiting for her there. . . .

She shook her head, and with hair flying, she ran. She must not, she must never allow herself to think these thoughts. That house was the only place on earth where she belonged. Suddenly, as if it were an omen, shining out to show her that she was right to think as she did, she saw the spotlight. Through the trees, there it was, bright and sharp and clear in the cold night. Her heart leaped with happiness and relief. Thank God, thank God, thank God, she had thought to turn the light on. This *was* her home, this *was* where she lived.

She raced from the lane and across the front yard scattering the drifts of leaves. In one motion she turned the key in the lock, banged open the front door, and sought the light switches. At her touch every light in the hall and the sitting room sprang on. She slammed the door and locked out the night.

The sitting room, though flooded with light, was empty and cold. She hurried to the hearth where the ashes lay white and gray. Too late to start a fire now, she thought. Her hand went to the mantelpiece and brought down her father's book which she took with her as she let herself fall back onto the couch.

Here, in the only place on earth where she belonged, she shivered.

The fear would not leave her.

She rose and went to the stairs, where she turned on the upstairs lights before reaching for the hall switch to plunge the downstairs into blackness.

Without a look into the parlor, she raced up the stairs.

Light spilled down the stairs into the hall and parlor. Then the pale glow from upstairs clicked off, shadows sprang forward and darkness swallowed the house. Only the front curtains, reflecting the spotlight, shone. Against this glow a shadow flickered.

The outside light went out.

20

WITH NO FIRE crackling on the hearth, no Gordon rattling in his cage, nothing in the cold parlor lived, nothing moved. Except for the girl in the bed upstairs, the house was as black as a silhouette, as dark and empty as the house down the lane. The wind scraped a maple branch across the roof. Far off in the night the ocean roared.

A key, unheard by the girl upstairs, clicked in the front door lock, a sound no louder than a blown leaf scratching at a window.

The door opened silently and the sharp, white beam of a flashlight sprang into the hall. A figure moved from the paler dark of the night sky into the house, soundlessly shut the door and locked it.

The wedge of light stabbed into the black of the sitting room and shot to the gateleg table and down to the braided rug. In total darkness except for the flashlight's beam, the figure moved into the room and almost noiselessly pulled the table from the rug. The rug was thrown back from the trap and the light found the hasp. A hand shoved the bolt back. The hinge on the door creaked, but that sound, like the others, was no more likely to arouse the girl upstairs than the tree branch clawing against the roof.

The light shining down the cellar steps suddenly swung across the room to the kitchen counter. The beam found the telephone.

The figure moved, grasped the instrument, carried it on its long cord to the cellar stairs, and moved downward, the flashlight beam casting descending pools of light.

The sitting room, almost black again, wavered in the faint light reflected from below. Sounds of footsteps and scrapings, covered by the wind would have gone undetected except for the telephone cord, that looped and caught on the trap, pulling the door shut with a slam.

The door pushed up, light stabbed out and swept the black room. Silently the door lowered shutting off all light.

Upstairs a light sprang on. Its glow spilled down the staircase where Rynn stood in bare feet, her white nightgown shining.

She stared into the dark. Her heart pounded, even though she told herself that, like the other sounds, the wind had made this one too. A broken branch had thudded against the house. That was it. Perhaps she had forgotten to lock the front door and it had blown open.

But she knew she had shut the door. Maybe a picture had fallen from the wall. The woodbox! Had she left the lid up? But the lid on the box made a different sound. What she had just heard was a heavier slamming. She fought accepting what she knew in her beating heart. *That sound.* She would never forget the first time she had heard that sound.

Noiselessly she ran down the stairs and across the hall to switch on the lights.

Nothing in the hall was out of place.

She dreaded looking into the parlor.

There it was, the one thing she dreaded to see more than

anything else in the world. The table stood to one side. The braided rug lay in a heap. There was the trapdoor.

Her mind raced. If she could break the terror which seized her, if she could move her shaking knees, if she could reach the trapdoor, she could bend the hasp back into place and throw the bolt. She could trap whoever was down there. *Then* she would have time to plan her next move. *Then* she could find out who it was. . . .

If she could move.

She fought the terror that held her locked. She fought to summon every ounce of effort.

Survive!

She broke her fear's hold and took the first step.

The second step followed. Too late. The hinges squeaked as the polished oak planks of the trapdoor before her began to rise.

She froze where she stood. The house filled with her screams.

The door pushed up, but no face appeared. Not even a hand was pushing up the trap. What was it, a stick? A cane. A black cane. As the door rose perpendicularly a black silk hat emerged, then a black cape, one arm of the cape covering the face.

"Mario!"

Suddenly released, suddenly able to move, Rynn sprang on bare feet across the cold floor.

"Oh, you bastard! You weren't sick at all! You only got your uncle, your brother and sister to help you pretend to be in hospital." Tears of incredulity and relief choked her as the words tumbled out. "And gray makeup, too? All this trouble so you could do this biggest magic trick of all?"

She laughed, a laugh that was out of control, but a laugh free from the rawness of cold fear.

"Oh you scared me!"

Her shoulders shook with silent laughter. She staggered toward the black cape rising from the steps, exultant in her release from terror, wild with joy. At the table she stopped, breathed deeply. She could play this game too, she could put on *her* act. With all the cold fury she was able to command, she shouted.

"You bloody bastard!" But unable to smother her joy, she burst into giggles and ran forward.

With the kind of wild theatrical gesture that capes and walking sticks inspire, the figure waited for the girl to run to his arms before he whirled around to face her.

This was not Mario's bright little face sparkling with black eyes and joyous smile, but the beefy red face and thick-lipped grin of Frank Hallet.

The man chuckled, "Your bloody bastard."

One pigskin hand pulled the trapdoor from the wall, and it dropped into place with a thud. The other held the telephone.

"Get out!" The trembling girl managed to rasp out the command.

Hallet pushed the telephone at her.

"Call the police." His grin cut a deeper crease across his red face. The man held out the receiver to emphasize his offer. He shook his head feigning surprise. No? He was saying, you don't want to use the telephone?

"Why don't you call your father?"

Cape swirling, he passed the girl and dropped the telephone on the counter. He glanced into the kitchen. "English and you're not going to offer me the obligatory cup of tea?"

"If you leave right now," Rynn said, her voice not much more than a whisper, "I won't say a word."

Hallet flourished his cape, enjoying its possibilities as if an amateur theatrical performance had presented him with the chance of new and more flamboyant personality. The cape responded wonderfully as he drew its length to his shoulder. With his other hand he tapped the cane on the floor.

"I only dressed up like this so if Fat-Ass Officer Ron Miglioriti or anyone else saw me come by—naturally they'd assume I was your little friend." He took a couple of uneven steps. "I even limp. You see?"

"Officer Miglioriti knows Mario's in the hospital."

He shrugged and rearranged the cape. "Ah—a slip up on my part. Fortunately there was no one to see me."

"Officer Miglioriti just brought me home from the hospital. He said he'd wait outside in the car until I signaled everything was all right."

"No more lies."

"He did. He promised to drive by and keep an eye on the house."

"Fat-Ass Ron Miglioriti is at his stupid raffle." Hallet looked annoyed as he gathered up a fold of black silk to brush away a smudge of white. "Dusty down cellar. Not just dust—what is it? Lye?" He scratched at the spot on his cape with a fingernail. "Down there, didn't know *what* I'd find. Probably because I didn't really know what I was looking for. Certainly not those dreary jelly glasses." Hallet flung back the black folds of the cape with a sweeping motion and held up a hand. Pinched between his thumb and forefinger was a small object which he thrust close to Rynn.

"Hairpin," he said. He leaned toward the girl, eyes scanning the length of her loose golden-brown hair. "But you don't wear hairpins, do you? Not in that pretty hair." He brought the tiny wire close for his own inspection. "Hairpin."

"Could have been down there for years," the girl said.

"But it would rust." He sniffed the wire and smiled. He

offered it to Rynn for examination, betraying no surprise when she shrank away.

"Still smells of the perfume I gave her for Mother's Day." He laughed. "Dear Mother." He unclosed his fist, displaying on the palm of his hand something even smaller than the hairpin.

"And this. Broken fingernail would you say? Bright red. Not Dear Mother's color at all. And here we also have these bits of hair. Now who do you suppose *they* belong to?" No miser ever turned his treasure in his hand with more fascinated greed, more love for what he held. "In the dark they were all I could find. The police—with all their equipment —no telling what they'll come up with." As if unwilling to part with his prizes, Hallet carefully placed them in a glass ashtray. He clapped his hands together, ready to take action.

"Shall we move the rug and the table back?"

He kicked the rug, shoving it over the trapdoor. With his foot he worked it, smoothing out the wrinkles, sliding it into place. He snapped his fingers at Rynn, and obediently she lifted one side of the table. With Hallet she carried the table back into place.

The man went to the back window where he parted the curtains and shaded his eyes to look out into the dark grape arbor.

"And how does your garden grow?"

At the table Rynn was placing the two pewter candlesticks in line.

"Out there," he said. "All that digging."

"Tulips," the girl said.

"Good. Dear Mother loves tulips." He let the curtains fall back into place. He pretended to be thinking aloud, but Rynn knew that just as he had indulged himself in the theatricality of the cape, hat and cane, he was playing to her now—a captive audience. "I suppose I should make an effort, but the truth is I don't really miss her all that much. You suppose that's very wicked of me? And as time goes on, I'm afraid I'm bound to feel even less of a sense of loss." He could not resist a grin as he slid chapstick across his lips. "No. I don't miss her, but the police seem to. . . ." He allowed his statement to trail off and hang; the words were spoken slowly, deliberately as like mist from his breath, in the cold air.

With her nail Rynn chipped a bit of candlewax from the tabletop.

"Remind me to think of her as I stand here—at this window—next spring at tulip time."

Here. Next spring. The words were spoken slowly, deliberately as he went to stand behind Rynn, who continued to scrape the wax from the tabletop.

"But I wouldn't for the world want you to worry about her. That's why I trudged over here." When Rynn would not face him, he circled her. Again she turned away.

"That's right, I walked. Aren't you going to ask why I didn't drive Dear Mother's lovely, liver-colored Bentley?"

He gathered his cape and strode past her to the fireplace. From the woodbox he produced some newspaper which he wadded and stuffed into the grate. He poked in kindling, lit the paper and watched the fire catch, his face reflecting the orange flames.

"Or don't you ask because you're so staggeringly brilliant that you know I don't want to leave it out in the lane for all the world to see? Right?"

He glanced up from the fire where the flames rose, licking at the kindling.

"Which reminds me. I owe you my thanks for bringing the car back to the office."

The girl stood at the table motionless, silent.

"Rynn?"

"I don't know what you mean."

"I mean you're brilliant. No two ways about it. But you made one mistake. I'm speaking of that famous Saturday she drove her pride and joy, her liver-colored Bentley, over here to pick up the equally famous jelly glasses. She never came home. But somehow her car did."

"That Saturday, she was never here."

"Now, you're being careless."

"She never came."

"My dear, I suggest you sit down."

Rynn made no move. Hallet snapped his fingers at the couch. He watched her as she sat, the firelight flickering on his face.

"She *did* come by. I know. I rode over with her."

In the silence she could hear him breathe.

"Now do you see why you must never make these careless statements?"

"She never came by."

"Don't be a bore. That Saturday I thought I'd visit you, too. As we left the office I lied. I told Dear Mother I wanted to see your neighbors before they closed up their house and went to Florida. Once we reached this lane she knew why I'd come out here. Dear Mother, she knew what I wanted. Parked right out there in front of this house we had the most terrible fight. She forbade me ever to come here again. She said she was going to talk with your father. Alone. About me —probably. You think it's too terribly paranoid of me to think that? It's true, however. No matter now. I waited for her to leave. And waited. In the rain remember? I saw you leave the house and come back. Saw the little lame magician bicycle up here and then bicycle away again. By then I was soaked through and trudged off home—leaving her car behind."

"None of that is true."

"You'll never know will you? If you ask Fat-Ass Officer Ron Miglioriti, you'll find out that the police left her Bentley, which I alone believed had so mysteriously reappeared at the office to sit there all day Sunday. Locked. Like a bank vault. Since Dear Mother had the only set of keys I was helpless to open the door. On Monday a tow truck dragged it off to Podesta's garage. You're supposed to be so brilliant, you tell me. How did I open the car door and start the motor without the keys?"

"She gave them to you."

"No, no, no," he said impatiently. "I told you, I haven't seen her. Besides, she wouldn't let me touch that precious car of hers."

"There was another set of keys?"

"When mother didn't want me to drive her car, you're saying she'd leave a set around for me to find? No way. No, Dear Mother was a very thorough woman. So—" He snapped his fingers for the girl's attention.

"So how did I open the door?"

"You called in a locksmith."

"*Voila!*"

"Then your mother still has the other set of keys."

"You're saying she drove back to the office?"

"Yes."

"And if not she, then who? Well, since you're such a staggeringly brilliant little girl I couldn't know for certain that you hadn't. It appears you are capable of the most remarkable things." He suppressed a giggle. "Once I had the doors open I scoured every inch of that car. Sherlock Holmes. Ellery Queen. Maigret, you name him. But I found nothing that said a little fourteen—or is it thirteen-year-old girl had driven the car. So, I looked again. You know what I found? On the plump leather paneling of the door were round marks. Thank God for real leather. Plastic wouldn't show them. Round marks from what? Round marks from the tip of a cane that someone had used to help get himself and something else out of the car? And in the back seat? Back there something had scratched Dear Mother's precious leather. Something that was too big to fit in the trunk? Also, more marks from a cane. Why? For support? Scratches—from a bicycle in the back seat? Round marks from putting a bicycle in, taking a bicycle out? The little lame magician? Up to his little lame tricks?"

The fire began to crackle.

"That was on Saturday. Unfortunately, I didn't get into the car till Tuesday. What did he do? Bring the keys back to you Saturday night? You have them now? On a chain around your pretty little neck?"

Hallet picked up the poker and stirred the fire. He lifted a maple log onto the flames.

"Of course that didn't tell me where Dear Mother was. That I still had to discover. Those evenings I came back here, I didn't drive." He sighed. "Oh, the times I trudged through the rain and autumn leaves just to see you. . . ."

He rose from the fire and brushed the soot from his hands. With exaggerated elegance, he drew his cloak around him and settled slowly into the rocking chair.

"There are a few details we still have to work out." He held up a cautioning hand. "Don't tell me. I'm enjoying doing this on my own far too much."

He snapped his fingers at the cigarette box. Rynn brought him the pack of Gauloise. He took one and waited. She struck a match and lit the cigarette for him. Inhaling, he leaned back and began slowly to rock.

"For fourteen—or is it thirteen—you *are* brilliant. Inventive. Resourceful. Cool under fire. But sooner or later all of us have to learn there are other brilliant people in the world. Discovering facts like that, I'm afraid, is part of grow-

ing up. Yes, it's sad not to be the center of the world any-
more, isn't it?"

Blue smoke curled around Hallet's pink face.

"You see, I know you finished Dear Mother off. Something to do with what she found down in the cellar. . . .
But, as I said, I'd rather leave the rest of it to talk about on
our long winter nights."

He reached forward and took the cigarettes the girl still
held in her hand.

"Pardon me. You want a cigarette? No?" He smoked,
maintaining his theatrical air.

"Don't look so solemn. I told you, I'm not angry with you
for getting rid of Dear Mother. A godsend. Saved me the
trouble. Hated the woman. Longed for some thunderbolt
to crash her down . . . some crab salad at a women's club
lunch to turn bad . . . some happy smashup on the express-
way to flatten that liver-colored Bentley like a duck press,
sending her blue blood trickling out in all directions. But
no. Every year she grew more healthy. Seemed to blossom.
My God, that woman was thriving on old age. I'd just about
given up hoping she'd *ever* kick off."

He smiled, mechanically rocking back and forth, like a
painted puppet in a toy chair, Rynn thought.

"So I say—*thank you*."

The telephone shrilled. Still smiling, the mechanical man
lifted a mechanical hand, ordering her to answer the telephone.

"Hello? Oh, Officer Miglioriti. Oh, I'm so glad you called."

Hallet rocked back and forth, his painted, glistening smile
unchanging.

"Well everyone *said* Mario's better. I didn't think—Yes?
Yes? He did? Thank goodness. I mean if that's what the doctor told his family, then I guess I shouldn't worry. Me? I'm
perfectly all right. Fine. I got the bus, just as you said . . .

What? Look, if it's really bad news perhaps now's not the time . . ."

She turned her back on the man in the rocking chair. The chair slowed its rocking and stopped.

"Yes," she said into the phone. "I see. Isn't that always the way? No. Not now. I mean I don't want to bother you. No really, I'll manage it. Thank you for calling."

She hung up.

The man by the fire blew out a long stream of smoke.

"Rule One," he said. "No secrets. Bad news?"

"I won the stupid Thanksgiving turkey."

"And you told him not to bring it by. Very wise."

Mechanically, Hallet began rocking.

21

"Tomorrow I'll go by the police station and pick up your turkey."

Hallet shook with a wheezy, silent laughter. "When I say your good-byes to Fat-Ass Ron Miglioriti for you."

He watched Rynn closely.

"Fat Ass is leaving us and going off to California."

Hallet, nodding and rocking, continued to watch the girl. But she showed no reaction.

"One less wop cop, right?" His wheeze bubbled into a hearty laugh. Only sucking on his cigarette quieted him. "As for the little magician, when he's out of the hospital we'll let you be the one to tell him. That will be your job, to tell him to go away and stay away."

Rynn, her arms across her nightgown, rubbed her elbows as she stepped back from the man.

"Where do you think you're going?"

"You asked for a cup of tea."

"England's answer to everything, right? Nice, hot cup of tea. First," he said, "put a record on. And turn down the lights."

Liszt surged into the house.

Enthroned in the rocking chair, Hallet was enjoying the ceremony he had staged, smoking with deliberate slowness as if he felt the world was waiting for his next imperial decree.

"I liked the way you handled yourself on the phone. Shows an innate capacity for learning. Except"—his pink face twisted on his thick neck to peer into the kitchen—"except for that one slip up about the car, you are—brilliant. Even better than brilliant. Smart. Clever. A survivor."

Survive.

From the tap, the girl was filling the kettle with hot water. She did not look at the man as she spoke.

"My father says that intelligence is the ability to see reality quickly."

"Does he? So does the famous American philosopher George Santayana, and unfortunately for your father, Santayana said it first." Hallet listened to the girl moving between the counter and the range. "At Harvard I majored in philosophy, that is, until I was kicked out. Oh, you're going to find me *full* of surprises."

Hallet rose from the chair, opened the woodbox and lifted out a maple log.

"No reason you shouldn't go right on the way you've been living. Only from now on, we'll be friends, you and I. Just we two. How does the song go? 'Nobody near us to see us or hear us.'" He was half singing, half talking the words and music of "Tea for Two." "'No friends or relations on weekend vacations—' Dear Mother loved, absolutely *adored* that song."

With a grunt he rolled the log into the fire.

"Mario," the girl said quietly.

"Yes?"

"He knows."

"Knows what?"

"What happened."

"As I said, we'll leave getting rid of him up to you."

"Maybe it won't be easy."

"Maybe he'll die."

"The doctors say not."

Hallet eased himself back into the chair.

"Then you'll simply have to use that brilliant little mind of yours and think of some way to let him know he's not wanted. Just let him drift away on his uneven little wop feet."

"Biscuits?"

"What?"

"You want biscuits?"

"But of course. Only here in the States we call them cookies."

The kettle whistled and then hissed as the girl lifted the boiling water from the range. She was filling the teapot when she said, "Mario's been down in the cellar."

"Busy place."

"As I said before, he knows."

"He a bright little wop is he?"

"Very."

"Then he'll be bright enough to know that he's an accomplice. You know that word?"

"Yes." She returned the kettle to the range.

"*He* knows what that means?"

"He'd know."

"He's the only other one who knows about the cellar?"

"Yes."

Hallet was studying the pack of Gauloise. Did he want another? At the sound of Rynn's footsteps he decided against the cigarette and watched the girl balance the tray on the corner of the coffee table as she knelt to the floor.

She pulled her bare feet under her as she cleared a place for the tea things. Hallet, an arm's length away, made no move to help. He stared at her hair glowing in the firelight.

"Mr. Hallet?"

"Yes, my dear?"

"You'll tell your wife?" The girl realized the risk the question carried. If, in this instant, the man had struck a stinging blow across her face, she would not have been surprised. But Hallet did not move.

"Suppose," he said, dropping all trace of banter, "you leave that to me."

Rynn moved saucers and cups, the teapot, the plate of cookies to the table. Hallet reached out a pink pigskin hand, his fingertips touching the spun-gold outline of Rynn's hair that shone in the glow of the fire.

"Pretty hair."

Rynn did not pull away from his touch. Instead she used the act of arranging the tea things to reach across the table to edge away almost imperceptibly from the man's hand. If Hallet saw her move as a withdrawal, he said nothing. He had time.

"Fire's catching," he said. "Nice and cosy now?"

Notes of the piano concerto fell like silver rain—a few notes shimmering at a time, building to that moment when a full shower of sound would burst.

"What are we listening to?" he asked.

"Liszt."

"Lovely." His eyes never left her.

"Milk?"

"Yes, please."

Hallet watched Rynn pour. With great skill she cut the flow of milk so neatly that not one extra drop spilled from the creamer.

"Sugar?"

"Go ahead. I'll tell you when."

She dropped in cubes of sugar till with a snap of his fingers Hallet stopped her.

"Three?"

"I'll expect you to remember that."

"That's easy," the girl said. "Same as I take."

Hallet tapped the table where he wished her to place the cup to be within reach at the rocker's forward tilt.

"Right there."

Rynn prepared her cup, the same amount of milk, three cubes of sugar.

"Nothing," the man said, "like a nice, hot cup of tea."

They listened to the music, neither touching the tea.

"Lovely," the man said.

"Mm."

After several minutes Hallet broke the silence.

"Something wrong, my dear?"

"No."

"Be honest now."

"It's just that it's a shame not to enjoy your tea while it's nice and hot."

"You mean, why don't I take my tea?"

"Not exactly."

"That is what you mean isn't it?"

"Yes, I guess—"

"You're not taking yours either."

"I'm waiting for you. You're the guest."

The man smiled. "You put more milk in yours."

"Did I?"

"Actually, that's the way I prefer mine."

"Here," the girl said lifting the creamer, ready to pour, "that's easy to make right . . ."

"I'd rather have yours," he said staring straight at her. He tapped the table and spoke with surprising harshness.

"When I talk to you, look at me."

Rynn lifted her green eyes to find his, but they faltered.

"I want *your* cup of tea," he said. "Gives us more a feeling of sharing, don't you think?" He reached out.

As Rynn raised the saucer and handed it to him she tried to keep the cup from chattering. In exchange Hallet slid his saucer and cup across the table.

"Don't wait for me," he said. "Ladies first."

Rynn lifted the cup.

"Wait."

She held the cup in mid air.

"Some English lady you are," he said wiggling his little finger at her. "You're not holding your pinkie out."

"I don't in England either," she said.

He watched her closely, waiting for her to take her first taste. She sipped the tea.

"Good?"

She took a longer sip. "As you say, nothing like a nice, hot cup of tea."

With her other hand she offered the man the plate and he took a cookie.

He broke the cookie with his teeth.

She waited as he tasted from his cup.

"Good." His lip balm's greasy mark glistened on the cup.

"Another biscuit?" she asked.

"The word is cookie," he said. "I told you that once." He coughed.

"The napkins," the girl said. "I'm afraid I've forgotten them. I'll get you one."

"Sit still."

"Enough milk?"

"Lovely." He sipped again. "You know why I made you change cups with me?"

"No." She knew at once he did not believe her.

"Think." His look demanded an answer.

"Some kind of test?"

"I switched those cups so you'll remember, when it comes to any little tricks, you'd do better to leave those to your little wop magician." He coughed.

Hallet crunched another cookie. He sipped more tea.

"Tea tastes of almonds."

Rynn felt the rough edge of her chipped tooth with her tongue as she bit into one of the cookies.

"I expect it's the almond cookies that give it that."

Hallet finished his tea and put the saucer on the table.

"You should see the way the fire lights up your hair. All brown and gold."

Over her teacup she watched the man lean toward her.

"Such lovely hair . . ."

Hallet's hand reached across the firelight to the girl. He stroked her hair. Rynn sat very still.